My Own Worst Enemy

Understanding and Overcoming Imposter Syndrome

Sydney Jackson-Clockston

© Copyright 2022 -Sydney Jackson-Clockston

All rights reserved.

The content contained within this book may not be reproduced, duplicated or transmitted without direct written permission from the author or the publisher.

Under no circumstances will any blame or legal responsibility be held against the publisher, or author, for any damages, reparation, or monetary loss due to the information contained within this book, either directly or indirectly.

Legal Notice:

This book is copyright protected. It is only for personal use. You cannot amend, distribute, sell, use, quote or paraphrase any part of the content within this book without the consent of the author or publisher.

Disclaimer Notice:

Please note the information contained within this document is for educational and entertainment purposes only. All effort has been executed to present accurate, up to date, reliable, complete information. No warranties of any kind are declared or implied. Readers acknowledge that the author is not engaged in the rendering of legal, financial, medical or professional advice. The content within this book has been derived from various sources. Please consult a licensed professional before attempting any techniques outlined in this book.

By reading this document, the reader agrees that under no circumstances is the author responsible for any losses, direct or indirect, that are incurred as a result of the use of the information contained within this document, including, but not limited to, errors, omissions, or inaccuracies.

Published by Stardust and Company Publishing LLC.

Paperback ISBN: 978-1-961870-00-0

Table of Contents

FOREWORD 1

A LETTER FROM THE AUTHOR 5

INTRODUCTION: STEPPING INTO YOUR POWER 9

CHAPTER 1: THE INS AND OUTS OF IMPOSTER SYNDROME .. 17

- WHAT IS IMPOSTER SYNDROME ANYWAY? 18
  - *The Fake, the Phony, and the Fraud* *19*
- WHY DOES IMPOSTER SYNDROME HAPPEN? 23
  - *Perfectionism* *23*
  - *Fear of Failure and Success* *23*
  - *Constant External Validation* *24*
  - *Lack of Praise* *24*
  - *Lack of Trust in Ourselves* *24*
  - *Lack of Authenticity* *25*
- WHO DOES IMPOSTER SYNDROME AFFECT? 25
- BREAKING YOUR GLASS CEILING 27
- CHAPTER ONE SOULWORK 29

CHAPTER 2: THE FIVE PILLARS OF IMPOSTER SYNDROME 31

- PERFECTION SYNDROME 32
- THE NATURALLY BORN EXCELLER 34
- THE LONE WOLF 36
- THE EXPERT 37
- THE SUPERHERO 38
- CHAPTER TWO SOULWORK 40

CHAPTER 3: FINDING CALM IN THE STORM 43

- WHAT IS CONTROL? 44
  - *Internal Locus vs. External Locus* *45*

UNDERSTANDING THE UNKNOWN 47
LOSING CONTROL IN THE MIDST OF FEAR....................................48
MASTERING YOUR EMOTIONS 50
   Give Yourself Space 50
   Become Self-Aware 51
   Name Your Emotion 52
   Acceptance..53
   Live in the Moment 54
CHAPTER THREE SOULWORK 55

CHAPTER 4: NAMING EMOTIONS 59

WHAT ARE EMOTIONS?..60
   The Happiness Drugs 60
   The Not-So-Great Chemical 61
   You Are The Boss! 61
RELEASING THE CHAOS 62
THE EMOTION WHEEL...63
CHAPTER FOUR SOULWORK 65

CHAPTER 5: ELIMINATING LIMITING BS 67

WHAT ARE BELIEF SYSTEMS?...68
   Your Belief Systems Can Impact Your Life 69
   Reframing Your Mindset...73
   Tools for Reframing Your Beliefs......................................75
CHAPTER FIVE SOULWORK 76

CHAPTER 6: FIXED MINDSET VERSUS GROWTH MINDSET 79

WHAT IS A FIXED MINDSET?..80
WHAT IS A GROWTH MINDSET? 81
WHAT HAPPENS NEXT?..83
   Affirmations 84
   Choosing Your Focus 84
   Mindfulness 85
CHAPTER SIX SOULWORK 85

CHAPTER 7: REDEFINING SUCCESS..89

DEFINING SUCCESS AS YOU GROW UP 90
EXTERNAL SUCCESS VERSUS INTERNAL SUCCESS.............................92

Copying Others' Success Is Not a Great Strategy—Here's Why 94
Defining Success Now 95
The Importance of Believing in You 98
Chapter Seven Soulwork 100

CHAPTER 8: SETTING SMART GOALS 103

What Are SMART Goals? 105
How Do You Create SMART Goals? *106*
Potential Obstacles and Solutions 110
The Cons *111*
The Pros *114*
Asking For Support 115
Taking Inspired Action 118
Journal About Your Goals *119*
Set Your Deadline *120*
Reframe Your Mindset *121*
The First Step Matters *121*
Keep Going *122*
Celebrate Your Accomplishments *122*
Chapter Eight Soulwork 123

GLOSSARY 135

REFERENCES 139

Foreword

The year was 1988, and in an instant, the reverberations of implicit bias steeped in the stench of systemic oppression, power, and privilege showed up...looking back, it was probably for the hundredth time. Still, at that moment, it felt like the impact was profound. At the ripe ol age of 15, I was awakened to the spirit of imposter syndrome. It is born out of the socialization of perfection and breeds a sense of ineptness. You see, education was important in my family. My late mother and father encouraged education and instilled values around education that I hold to this day. Like many individuals, especially those with marginalized identities, I was told by a school counselor to take a trade and that I wasn't college material. Essentially the message was... you aren't good enough. You aren't perfect. You are stupid...so don't bother.

Trades are wonderful! There is absolutely nothing wrong with a Trade. In some cases, you can earn as much or more with a trade as you can in professions that require a degree. But for the person that wanted one of those degree-required professions, it was a dream crusher. The imposter lie also birthed a fear that became a factor fueled even more by an ableist society. Living with unseen disabilities presented its own challenges, and a battle for my self-worth ensued.

I knew in 3rd grade that I wanted to be a teacher. I just felt the passion for it in my soul. I also vividly remember my third-grade teacher and all that Patrica Kulp, my 3rd-grade teacher, poured into me as a child. I never knew I would draw on the seeds of love that a teacher planted in my soul or the time my mother spent playing school with me to inspire the fire to teach inside of me as the imposter lie had tried to snuff it out. Life is scorched in ways that can sometimes be surreal for many of us. Historical trauma, generational oppression, abuse of power… and then there is hope in those moments when you meet someone so magnificent that they will forever change your life and its' trajectory for the better.

That happened to me. It was the year 1991, New Year's Day, to be exact. A pivotal time… for ahh Starr was born. Literally! Author, speaker, coach, travel specialist, natural resources and sustainability expert, ahhhhhmazing human and magnificent solopreneur, and more, Sydney Starr came into my life as a gift of splendor. She has added to this plant profoundly, changing lives for good. Her work in so many areas is done with such integrity and implemented with groundedness and grace. As a child, it was Sydney Starr who, in her own third-grade experience, advocated for herself as a person with dyslexia. Through my years of watching and learning from my little Sydney as she led by example, advocating for herself in the same education system, I navigated. That I was inspired to tell myself louder than the echoes of imposter lies that I should and could. Seeing Sydney navigate the education system was like a fresh awakening and inspiration. She let nothing stop her. Fast forward, I have lived through a host of challenges, overcome a lot, and earned my highest degree, a doctoral one. Still, to this day, I must affirm my inner power.

Through my coaching sessions with Sydney, I have learned to lean into why imposter syndrome happens. I normalized that it is not just in my head but a real phenomenon many people deal with across a spectrum. I discovered the pillars that prop this wreck-lose minduck up, analyzed how to deal with the dread that can paralyze productivity, and designed a plan that supports introspection and constructs self-trust. Now as you peruse the pages of this insight-filled book, you can make an action plan to combat the imposter lie that lurks around in a failed attempt to oppress your greatness.

You have indeed made this world better than it was before you entered it. Thank you, Sydney Starr, child of mine!

Dr. Julie Clockston, LCSW, Cert ED
Doctor of Social Work
Assistant Professor & Solopreneur

A Letter From the Author

To the person reading this right now,

I found myself having another out-of-body experience. No, I wasn't on drugs. I just felt stuck and unhappy. While sitting in my home office, I was trapped on yet another conference call for work. This call literally meant nothing to me. I felt nothing.

As I sat on this call, my eyes half glazed over, and I swear, I astral projected for a few moments. I was thinking to myself, "What the fuck are you doing with your life? Why are you wasting your time here? You know your opinion isn't valued. You know they see you only as the help." I had taken this job and all that came with it, including a pay cut, thinking that I was going to be on a small team with nice people. I was going to be working with local businesses and helping them raise money for a local charity. I was going to be doing my part to make a difference in the world. Unfortunately, it ended up being another job that cared more about making a profit; even fundraising was all about winning and making money for the benefit of the company and nothing else. Needless to say, it was a toxic environment to be in.

I had a slew of other toxic work experiences. In one of my other positions, I allowed the General Manager, who was a mean drunk, to mistreat myself and other staff. When I finally chose to stand up and speak out about the sexual harassment and racist remarks, I was given the silent treatment, which is just another form of abuse, if you ask me. Fast forward many years, I accepted another position that I thought was going really well. This company ended up cutting my pay, simply due to the societal and political power they felt they had over me. It didn't matter if I achieved the highest rating amongst all of the staff. They took advantage of my help and diminished it at the same time.

Each of these situations triggered an out-of-body experience. I finally asked myself, "Why? Why do you allow yourself to be treated this way? You have a wealth of knowledge; even more than your superiors. Why do you allow them to diminish your light and dull your sparkle? Why do you keep telling yourself you're not good enough or that this is the best it's ever going to get? Why don't you just start your own business? Why?"

Omigosh, the list of whys just kept coming. I once thought I was working in my career, but due to the self-doubt and confidence I had in my abilities as well as the mental abuse I received from my superiors, it quickly became a job that I hated with a passion. I started to write down all the whys floating in my head, and they lingered in my mind so strongly. It came to the point where I finally had a breakthrough. I discovered what I wanted out of my life. I desire to leave a legacy. Omigosh, I wish I knew what that is though. I just knew that what I was doing would not get me there. So, I made a courageous decision for myself, and I quit. I resigned from my position and walked away from everything that kept me in survival mode–my bi-weekly paycheck, health insurance, matching IRA, sick days, and vacation days. I walked away from pending contracts that I knew would bring in an extra $2,500-$5,000. None of this stopped me from going after what I wanted. I knew my mental health was more important than any of it.

During this journey, I struggled with imposter syndrome, and I didn't even realize it. I wished that I had a resource, such as this book, to aid me through the struggle on the road to discovering myself. If I was feeling this way, I knew that there were others with a similar struggle. I knew that it was imperative that I create a tool to help others who feel stuck and unfulfilled in life like I once did. I know there are many other folks out there who also worry that they are never going to get to where they want to be in life. This book is for those of us who are sick and tired of being sick and tired. Fasten your seatbelt and get ready to step into your own greatness.

I would be remiss not to pay acknowledgment to the folks who have supported me each step of the way. I first want to thank my mom, Dr. Julie Clockston. Thank you for always praying for my success in life. I am blessed to have a mother like you to learn from. We don't always agree, but I can always count on your support and love in all of my endeavors.

Thank you to my partner, Matt McCalla. You have been an integral part of my success. You have always filled my head with positive encouragement to be an entrepreneur. I am so fortunate to have a partner who does this when I know that it is not the case for most people. Of course, I cannot forget the rest of the squad in my life that continues to root for my success. Thank you, Raeven-Lynn, Mark Jr., Jayden, Theresa, and Ollie. You all believed in me, even when I didn't believe in myself.

Passion Over Perfection,

Sydney Jackson-Clockston

Introduction:

Stepping Into Your Power

"The exaggerated esteem in which my lifework is held makes me very ill at ease. I feel compelled to think of myself as an involuntary swindler." –Albert Einstein

You are your own worst enemy. I know how this sounds but hear me out. You are your best friend, but at times, you are also your bully. You are the one who, when you feel like it, will cheer you on and support you like crazy. You feel on top of the world, but then again, there's this other part of you. It is the one who beats you up when you feel down and tells you that you are a fake. An imposter. A lowly servant. A fraud. A pretender. An impersonator. The one who makes you hide most of the time.

You could be doing so well at your job, helping people and doing your part to make the world a better place to live in, but then, a seemingly dark cloud looms over you. It hits you like a ton of bricks. *What the heck are you doing? What's wrong with you? What's the point of all this? One day, people will notice that you don't belong here. That you are a fake. You better quit before this happens.*

And so, you do.

You go back to your hiding place, hoping to never be found again. You blend in so you don't stick out like a sore thumb. You forget it all–your passions, your purpose, your excitement, the abundance you're chasing, your joy, your resilience–all because the bully inside of you told you it wasn't worth it.

Welcome to imposter syndrome.

If this resonates with you, I want you to know something. The version of you that is quietly shouting all of the nasty comments from inside of you is only trying to protect you from both real and perceived harm. Overtime, your lived experiences have resulted in Negative BS (belief system). One byproduct of a negative BS is imposter syndrome which psychologically keeps you safe from the risk of failure and the risk of success. Unfortunately, imposter syndrome also keeps you oppressed with possible feelings of being stuck, low self-confidence, worthlessness, anxiousness, overwhelm, and depression.

Imposter syndrome happens to the best of us. Many of the celebrities you know and love today have experienced imposter syndrome at least once in their lifetime. Every time they make a movie, or sing another song, or invent some extraordinary thing, they feel like an imposter; but yet, they move forward and do it anyway. Even though it keeps splashing ice cold water in their face, telling them to wake up from this dream.

Imposter syndrome is not something that occurs overnight, which is why it takes a conscious effort to stop it from being our default BS and mindset.

Dismantling imposter syndrome is a process, and for some, it's a lifelong journey. This book is a supportive tool for you to use throughout your journey. My hope is that this book not only educates and brings clarity into your life, but it also uplifts and empowers you to discover your inner light and develop a healthier belief system and mindset.

You may not fully understand that you are struggling with imposter syndrome, and that's okay. This is why this book exists. If you're reading it right now, it's because the universe has led you to this moment. The universe is telling you that you're ready for change and transformation. It's telling you that you are already an overcomer the moment you flipped to the first page.

Believe me, I do not take your story lightly. I am a certified coach, public speaker, and author, yet I've experienced imposter syndrome more times than I count. I know what it feels like to wake up every morning, wanting to do good and help, but battle with feeling like a fraud every single day. It's not fun, but if I can overcome it, so can you.

Throughout my own experience with imposter syndrome, there are a few things that I learned that I know can help you:

- **Understand how imposter syndrome shows up in your life.** This is the first step. I'm talking about pure self-awareness. Becoming consciously aware that you struggle with imposter syndrome. The moment you are aware, the moment your life starts to change.

- **Understand that you have an incredible gift.** You may be a coach, like me, or a baker, singer, artist, author, or accountant. Your gift matters in this world. To help combat imposter syndrome, you need to own and embody your gifts for all their worth.

- **Self-trust is the only thing that should matter to you.** Everything else will fall into place and align the moment you declare that you trust yourself.

- **Your inner circle matters more than you know.** Do they support you or criticize you? This makes a world of difference. Go where you're celebrated, not tolerated.

There are many other things that I can share with you, and I will, but they will be sprinkled throughout this book. As you read, I want you to remember something: If you want to truly change your life, you need to take the first step. You need to take the actions you're scared of taking. That's the beauty of this journey. It may not be easy, it may be difficult, but it's definitely worth it. You'll need to stretch yourself as far as you possibly can in order to get to where you want to go. You'll need to step into the most uncomfortable parts of your journey, but that's okay–you have the courage, perseverance, and determination to do so. It's all within you. It's up to you to achieve extraordinary things.

Think of this book as your success toolkit. It is your guide and your coach. It will teach you things that you may not even be aware of. Some of the incredible takeaways that are ready for you to learn are:

- The five pillars of imposter syndrome and how to identify and cope with them.

- How to gain control of your life again simply by letting go (I know this may sound odd, but believe me, it's worth the read.)

- Understanding your emotional rollercoaster.

- How to eliminate the limiting BS (no, it's not the BS you're thinking, although it's similar.)

- How to expand your mind in the most extraordinary way.

- How to find incredible, unique success in your life where you're feeling complete fulfillment and passion.

You will notice, at the end of each chapter, I provide you with what I call *'soulwork'* and journal prompts. Soulwork is essentially homework but completed on a deeper level. At school, you do homework to get a good grade and to complete a task you were assigned. Think of soulwork as doing homework from the spirit; the grade is considered your transformation, and the task is going through spiritual reflection.

Apart from the soulwork, you will also be asked to complete journal prompts. Please do not skip these, as it's all a part of your journey to personal transformation. The pen is mightier than the keyboard, so I highly suggest getting a journal specifically for meditation and handwriting everything.

Your journal does not have to be fancy at all. It could be as simple as a spiral notebook.

You may ask why handwrite? It comes down to a science discovered in a study published in *Psychological Science*. Researchers found that students who take notes by hand tend to learn more than those who type their notes on a laptop. Why? Since people can type faster than they can write, they are also able to take down all or most of the information presented without having to filter it. You may think that a major advantage of this is that, on the surface, you're getting more info down on paper; however, there is a disadvantage. Since students who write their notes by hand cannot write everything down, they have to be more selective. While they take their notes, they have to process the information on the spot to decide what is important enough to write down and what they can leave out.

It can also be said that they have to process enough information to be able to summarize their notes in fewer words. This extra round of information processing helps make it more memorable, so those who write their notes tend to have a better understanding of the subject matter. It's as if they're completing an extra round of studying each time they take notes.

I could go on and on, but then I'll steal the thunder from the rest of the book. To conclude, I want you to flip to chapter one with this in mind: Imposter syndrome is not the end. Just like a doctor says to their patients, there is a long road ahead, but it's not impossible. With strength, determination, resilience, and perseverance, you can heal. In due time, you will be unstoppable again.

I'll see you on the other side.

Chapter 1:

The Ins and Outs of Imposter Syndrome

"Do not ever let anyone make you feel like you don't matter, or like you don't have a place in our American story—because you do. And you have the right to be exactly who you are." –
Michelle Obama

There may be moments in your business, career, relationships, finances, passion, purpose, or personal and spiritual growth that you feel like a fraud. You may feel like everyone is better than you. You may feel like their gifts are important, but what's the point of yours? You may be asking yourself, "What makes me so special?" and you trudge through your life asking yourself that very question every single day, never coming up with the answer.

You are experiencing imposter syndrome, but you may not be consciously aware that you are. This chapter will break it down for you.

Chances are that you have an idea of what imposter syndrome is, but you may not know how and why you struggle with it in the first place. This chapter will be an eye-opener for you. It will be a moment in your life during which time will stand still because you finally realize where it stems from. This chapter will bring the subconscious knowing of imposter syndrome out into the open so you can have one of your biggest 'a-ha' moments ever. I guarantee your life is about to change.

What Is Imposter Syndrome Anyway?

According to *verywellmind.com*, "Impostor syndrome is an internal, psychological experience in which one believes that they are not as competent as others perceive them to be, as if they are a fraud" (2022). In other words, you feel like a phony. It doesn't matter if there is extraordinary evidence of your success and accomplishments; you still feel there is nothing special about you. It's like you don't deserve any of the success you've achieved and continue to achieve.

Many people have experienced a short burst of imposter syndrome. Usually, this is seen in your business or job. As you get settled and acquainted in your role, imposter syndrome will rear its ugly face. You feel like you don't know what you're doing. You feel like your co-workers have more experience than you. At some point during the transition, you wonder why you ever got hired or launched your business in the first place. It doesn't matter how much success you already have under your belt, you still feel like an imposter in a successful body. So often, imposter syndrome sheds as we become more comfortable in our role, start to feel like we fit into the culture, and build connections. However, living with imposter syndrome is like repeating that doubt every day for an extended time period.

Some of the symptoms of imposter syndrome are:

- Self-doubt
- Negative self-talk
- Anxiety
- Depression
- Nervousness
- External validation
- People-pleasing
- Fear of failure
- Self-sabotage
- Self-judgment

The Fake, the Phony, and the Fraud

To help describe imposter syndrome even further, I want to share a fun little short story with you about three ladies who had amazing things to offer, but because of imposter syndrome, they didn't see it for themselves.

Once upon a time, there were three beautiful Queens–Queen Fake, Queen Phony, and Queen Fraud. All three Queens were not only allies; they were the best of friends. Each royal subject in their kingdom adored them. They had a kind heart, they were fair to their subjects, and they had so much to offer their people. However, even though they were adored by their kingdoms and their people looked up to them, they were not doing so well on the inside. Each queen felt like they didn't matter, and they were never good enough. They constantly doubted their decision-making skills and they spent a lot of time visualizing how things could get better, and if things didn't feel like they were getting better, they would blame themselves.

When a member of their court would offer them compliments, telling them they're beautiful or smart, they would simply dismiss the compliment and immediately think it was an obligatory pleasantry. "They're supposed to say that," they thought. Even though a member would tell them that they're the best Queen they've ever had, they wouldn't believe them and still doubt their ability and intelligence. Each Queen had so much difficulty receiving compliments. Of course, as time went on, their self-doubt and anxiety began to grow. To themselves, they were small and inadequate. They weren't fit to be a Queen.

Their confidence began to dwindle little by little and soon, they were talking negatively about themselves, and the joy in their life became non-existent.

Queen Fake: "It is only a matter of time before my kingdom learns the truth. I have no idea what I'm doing. There's no manual on running a kingdom."

It didn't matter how much knowledge she acquired as she trained to be a Queen since she was a little girl; her mantra was still, "Fake it until you make it." She constantly thought, "My success is a total fluke. I've just been lucky to have made it this far." As a means to distract herself and to try and prove that she has something to offer her people, she started to help her royal subjects with their duties, and she volunteered in the kingdom as much as she could. One of her downfalls as a Queen was to take on anything and everything because she had difficulty relinquishing control. "If you want something done right, you have to do it yourself." She lived by this every single day.

Queen Phony: "The weight of the world is on my shoulders. I need to be and do everything I can so I can pave the way for future queens."

Queen Phony's people loved and adored her. They even wished to create a glorious parade in her honor. However, her royal advisors would constantly belittle her and point out her flaws when she made mistakes. It didn't feel nothing was ever good enough for them. She couldn't live up to their standards and expectations. Very soon, their comments began to deteriorate her, and she started feeling like a fraud. She dwelled on every single error she made. As she witnessed her own parade, she couldn't let go of the fact that she felt like a failure. She didn't believe that she deserved a parade in her honor, let alone to be a queen. Sadness consumed her daily life and she felt worthless and never enough.

Queen Fraud: "I love my best friends so much, but I feel like I am their shadow. Queen Fake is so successful because she volunteers in her kingdom. I don't do that.

That's probably why I'm not as successful as she is. Queen Phony's subjects love her so much that they threw her her own parade. That's never happened to me. I feel like such a loser."

Queen Fraud has received so many compliments and acknowledgements from the people in her kingdom, but yet, she still compared herself to her friends and didn't believe she had anything good to offer. She is so creative, but she was always afraid of following up on her ideas. She always did things halfway. She constantly compared her reign and her kingdom to what her friends were doing and did what she could to mirror their success. If they created extraordinary programs, she would attempt to copy them in hopes hers would be successful too, but, of course, success doesn't work this way, and the programs didn't take off as much as she expected them to. Queen Fraud saw this as evidence that she really was a failure. She allowed her emotions and negative self-talk to control her life and she went into hiding. She allowed her advisors to make all of the decisions and implement new ideas. "This is so much better than failing–yet again."

Now that you've read these little stories of these Queens, I want you to do some reflection: Do you see yourself in any one of these Queen's stories? If so, which one? How does her story resonate with you? Once you become self-aware of which Queen's shoes you are currently filling, you'll be able to see where you can make some changes in your own personal growth and confidence.

Why Does Imposter Syndrome Happen?

Here's an interesting fact: Around 70% of people have imposter syndrome at some point in their lifetime (zapier.com, 2017).

Imposter syndrome can occur in our lives because of a few reasons:

Perfectionism

We feel the need to be perfect all the time. Doing things imperfectly will never feel good enough. It's as if we believe that people have high expectations of us; therefore, if we don't live up to their expectations, we feel like a fraud. We have this perfect little vision of the way we want things done and if it happens in a way we least expect it to, we feel like a failure.

Fear of Failure and Success

Every time we hit a milestone or accomplishment, we don't feel like we deserve it. We feel like it wasn't supposed to be that way and we have a fear that people will find out we created success as a fraud, and it will be taken away from us. We have such high expectations of who we are, and we are terrified of failing. If we fail, we believe that to be evidence that success is not meant for us, and we are trying to prove something about us that is not actually true.

Constant External Validation

We are always seeking approval from others. If we are not feeling praised by others, we feel like a failure and an imposter. If someone doesn't recognize what we are doing, we use that as evidence that no one cares and that they're probably not recognizing us because they see us as a fake.

Lack of Praise

If we didn't receive praise from our parents or elders, especially during our childhood, we would grow up to believe that it's because we didn't do anything special, and that's the belief that our subconscious mind would embody.

Lack of Trust in Ourselves

We may feel we are never good enough for anything or anyone. We may feel like an imposter at work because we believe we don't have the skills, wisdom, and knowledge to live up to the expectations of our role. We may constantly doubt ourselves in our abilities and believe that we don't have anything good to offer the people around us. We may have a lack of confidence when it comes to completing projects, with the belief that someone could do a better job and that we don't have enough knowledge to complete the project.

Lack of Authenticity

Simply put, imposter syndrome dulls our sparkle. We may believe that we are not unique, and we've lost our identity in the world. Because of this, we lack luster and shine, and we feel like we need to constantly prove ourselves to everyone. We try to copy others in an attempt to feel successful, just as they are, but in the end, we still feel like a failure. We forget the importance of sharing our unique voice and message with the world. Instead, we hide because we believe no one cares what we have to say because we are not as successful as the person beside us.

There are many reasons why imposter syndrome exists in our lives. In order to truly release it, it is important to become aware of why it exists in your life and to find a way to rectify it so you can believe in yourself and your abilities even more.

Who Does Imposter Syndrome Affect?

Imposter syndrome can happen to anyone. There is no specific gender, financial status, or education status that it targets. However, imposter syndrome has been known to affect many people who have extraordinary accomplishments. It also affects more women than men. There are many individuals who have amazing knowledge, they studied multiple degrees, they have written books and helped a lot of people but yet, they still feel like a fraud. They still have a tremendous fear that someone is going to find out they are a fake and the accomplishments they bring to the table are not actually true.

There are many millennials who are also affected by imposter syndrome. According to *thewalrus.ca*, about one third of millennials are affected and feel like a fraud (2022). This usually happens because they didn't receive praise or appreciation during their childhood, or they were raised by their parents to be a perfectionist in everything that they do. They step into adulthood feeling like everything they do is never good enough, or they're not doing enough; therefore, they feel like a fraud.

Imposter syndrome disproportionately affects women, especially women of color. There are many times where a woman will feel unheard, unacknowledged, or unseen at home or in their workplace, which can lead to feelings of unworthiness and doubt and lead towards feeling like a fraud.

"We're more likely to experience imposter syndrome if we don't see many examples of people who look like us or share our background who are clearly succeeding in our field." – Emily Hu

Imposter syndrome can hit them hard and last for weeks or even months due to the fact that they:

- **Take on more that they can handle.** When they begin to feel overwhelmed or stressed, they feel they're not doing enough or feel like a failure.

- **Attribute all of their success to luck.** Any accomplishments they have, they rarely feel it's because of all their hard work, but rather that it's because they were simply 'lucky' or because they believe that other people created their success.

- **Doubt all they have to offer.** They don't trust themselves or they lack confidence; therefore, they don't feel anything good can come out of their efforts.

- **Dislike what they are doing.** They feel overwhelmed, burned out, or exhausted because they are not happy in their current job or business. Because of this, they feel like an imposter and even more of a failure because they are not doing what they are passionate about.

Breaking Your Glass Ceiling

The first step to breaking your struggle with imposter syndrome is to become aware that it is happening in the first place. Knowledge is power; therefore, if you are not aware that you feel this way, you will not be able to take action to rectify it and move forward.

I would also like to personally acknowledge how strongly imposter syndrome can affect women and others in the BIPOC (Black, Indigenous and People of Color) community.

If you reside in the USA, it is important to understand and remember that we live in a patriarchal and racist society. Our social system is set up in a way where Caucasian men not only primarily hold power, but also have dominant political roles of leadership. They are known to hold the keys to moral authority, social privilege, and control of property. This forces successful, accomplished men and women, such as us, to fight against the society we were raised in. The society that is meant to keep us small and concealed, as we are meant to "stay in our own lane and remember where we stand in status."

However, all of these limitations are making us stronger in order to break one glass ceiling after another. When I worked in the corporate world, I couldn't help but notice that I was often the only woman. I was not only the only black person, but I was also the youngest person in the room when it came to management status. In my last job, I found myself getting picked on for my spelling and grammar, even though I constantly communicated that I was dyslexic.

I also remember, one day when I was late for a meeting, my boss gave me a huge lecture because I got lost in a place I've never been before, but here's the most ironic thing: The exact same mistakes I was constantly being picked on and berated for were being frequently made by my boss. It was because of examples like this that I felt like I was being misunderstood, and I didn't feel seen, which then made me feel like a failure.

Women not only combat limiting beliefs about themselves, but also limiting beliefs that come from others. Regardless of how imposter syndrome gets in a woman's head, they owe it to themselves to better understand the limiting beliefs and how they manifested so she can take her power back and reshape them into positive beliefs.

If we're experiencing a huge fear of failure, it is our responsibility to understand the root of where this fear comes from so we can release it and experience freedom from it. If we struggle with self-doubt, we have the power within us to combat it and grow our confidence. It is up to us to change our lives, but first, we need to understand how to; everything else will follow.

Chapter One Soulwork

If you enjoy journaling, I have a few journal prompts about this chapter I'd like to share with you. If you have never journaled before, this is a great time to start.

These are beautiful reflection exercises that will help you take inspired action as you begin to become aware of how imposter syndrome is affecting you:

1. Did you learn something new about imposter syndrome?

2. Did anything in the short story about the Queens stand out to you?

3. How do you feel the Queens are stuck in imposter syndrome? What characteristics of imposter syndrome do you believe they have?

4. Are there any characters from the story that you relate and resonate with? Who is she, and how can you relate to her?

5. Do you have imposter syndrome? If yes, what characteristics of imposter syndrome do you believe you have?

6. What is your "truth" that you are worried people will discover about you?

7. Do you believe you are stuck in the imposter syndrome cycle? How do you feel you can get out of it?

8. How has imposter syndrome held you back in your personal and professional life?

9. Have you ever had someone plant a seed of doubt in your head? What did you do to overcome it? If you haven't overcome it yet, what do you feel is the next step in order to do so?

Chapter 2:

The Five Pillars of Imposter Syndrome

"It's almost like the better I do, the more my feeling of inadequacy actually increases, because I'm just going. Any moment, someone's going to find out I'm a total fraud." –Emma Watson

There is a reason why imposter syndrome exists in our lives. In fact, there are MANY reasons. In chapter one, we spoke briefly about the main reasons; in this chapter, we'll be discussing the main personality types that are most often associated with imposter syndrome.

Many don't realize that imposter syndrome tends towards five major personality types. As you read through them, you may notice that you resonate with one, a few, or all of them. Knowing about these personality types is imperative because then, you'll be able to rectify your imposter syndrome based on where you fall in the personality types.

Perfection Syndrome

Being a perfectionist and feeling like an imposter is connected at the hip. If you are a perfectionist, you are usually ensuring everything in your life has to be perfect. If it isn't, you feel disappointed and experience massive self-doubt. You lose trust in yourself and constantly beat yourself up as you question why things didn't work the way you expected them to. You set massive goals and expect to accomplish them, but if you don't, you feel like a failure and have difficulty getting back on track. If you like things perfect, you're usually doing every single task yourself, as you have trouble relinquishing control and allowing people to help.

It's usually simple to understand if you're a perfectionist, as the behaviors are easy to identify, but at times, you may be too wrapped up in your perfectionism to notice. If this is the case and you're wondering if you fall in this category, you can ask yourself some reflection questions in your journal:

- Do you find yourself micromanaging others?

- Are you usually a backseat driver when it comes to control?

- Do people try to help you with tasks, but you find yourself saying, "I can do it myself," even if you really could use the extra support?

- When you set high goals and you don't accomplish them within the expected timeframe, do you feel guilty or shameful? Do you beat yourself up and feel you don't have enough knowledge to accomplish the goal, otherwise you would have accomplished it?

- Do you enjoy things in your personal and professional life a certain way? For example, your house is always neat and tidy (almost perfect), the items on your desk look perfect, and not a single thing is out of place?

- Do you set high expectations for yourself, and if it's not 100%, you feel frustrated and question your ability and whether you know enough?

- Do you have trouble letting go?

- Are you terrified of failing?

All of these questions can help you decipher whether you struggle with perfectionism. Although they're "yes" or "no" questions, I encourage you to dig deeper with your answers. Diving deeper into knowing yourself and your flaws can help you understand the root of where your struggle with imposter syndrome comes from. Understanding that you're a perfectionist only scratches the surface–the root of why you're a perfectionist is still yet to be discovered.

The Naturally Born Exceller

You have an inner belief that you need to excel at everything you do. You believe that you need to be naturally gifted at many, if not all, things in your life. If you're not, you judge and criticize yourself, especially if it takes you a long time to excel at something. Similar to being a perfectionist, you usually put high expectations on yourself to be extraordinary, and if you don't master something on the first try, you push yourself harder and judge yourself for not doing things as great as others.

You may compare yourself to many others around you, especially those who seem to be good at everything they do. You don't understand why you can't be like them, and you question your worthiness or sufficiency. You are someone who has a niche or a few niches that you excel at effortlessly. As these niches seem to come easy for you, self-judgment is usually the first thing that shows up in your life when you are not able to get things done right off the bat.

Most of us naturally excel at many things in our life. There is a difference when imposter syndrome gets in the way of feeling naturally gifted and borderline perfectionistic. We can feel like an imposter, even when we are naturally gifted at something. Perhaps we notice someone who has similar gifts; therefore, we feel like we are unable to compete. We can also feel like a fake because we want everything to be perfect. When it's not, we don't feel we're good enough and there is someone out there who could probably do things better.

Some reflection questions you can ask yourself in order to understand if you fall under this category are:

- Is accepting challenges a struggle for you because you fear you won't excel at them?

- How strongly do you dislike not mastering something on the first try?

- Do people usually acknowledge your efforts, and when you don't master what they're referring to, you feel intense guilt or shame? Does it make you want to hide?

- If you don't master something right away, do feelings of unworthiness or not feeling enough show up?

- Have people raved about your intelligence, but a setback happens that makes you question its truth?

- As a child, were you usually excelling at every grade with A+ across the board? If you received a lower grade, did you find yourself questioning your intelligence and feel shameful because of it?

The Lone Wolf

"I can do everything myself." This is the phrase that The Lone Wolf loves to use. You rarely ask for help when you're struggling, and when you do, you feel like a failure, ego sets in, and shame gets in the way. You feel that if you're not independent, you're not worthy, and if you're not worthy, you're not enough.

If someone offers you help, you feel ashamed and offended; it's as if someone just told you that you don't know what you're doing, so you feel insulted. You do everything in your power to become 'self-made' so that you can take pride in your success, but what you tend to neglect is that there is always a team supporting you behind-the-scenes.

In order to figure out if The Lone Wolf characteristic is a part of who you currently are, there are a few questions you can reflect on:

- Do you always feel that you can do everything yourself?

- Do you get annoyed or frustrated when someone offers their help? Do you feel that, maybe, your ability is being questioned?

- Do you struggle with asking for help in fear that you failed at the task?

- Do you have a hard time relinquishing control and working with a team because your ego tells you to do it all yourself?

The Expert

You always believe that you are never enough. What you know, the accomplishments you've acquired, who you are, what you do—you feel it is never enough. Your expertise or success is usually determined by everything you know and everything you don't know. For example, you constantly question whether you know enough. One of your biggest fears is that people will find out that you don't have as much knowledge as you say you do and will judge and criticize you.

You also tend to be mindful in what you're doing, as you fear you are not enough as you are—you stop yourself from applying for jobs, you choose not to go after the promotion at work, and you don't start your dream business—this is all because of the constant phrase replaying in your mind: "What if I am not enough?" or, "What if I don't know enough?" This is a vicious cycle that leads to self-sabotage, constant imposter syndrome, and lack of confidence in your abilities.

Some reflections you can ask yourself in order to understand if you demonstrate this trait are:

- Do you find yourself self-sabotaging constantly in your career or business?

- Do you constantly use the phrase, "I am not enough," in many instances, such as a job, business, or relationship?

- Are there many training sessions that you have signed up for because you feel that once you take that training, you'll have more than enough skills and knowledge?

- Does it make you nervous when someone calls you an 'expert' or tells you that you have so much wisdom and knowledge? Does it make you feel ashamed?

The Superhero

Throughout your daily life, you do all that you can to try and prove your worth to others. You are always the first to arrive at work and the last one to leave. You usually take on more projects than you can handle and do extra homework at school. Even though people may sing your praises, you still feel more inadequate than others.

Imposter syndrome takes a huge precedence in your life, as you always find it extremely hard to measure up to others, regardless of your skills, accomplishments and knowledge. You never feel you're good enough; therefore, you push yourself to do better every single day. Because of this, you are a severe workaholic and neglect having a personal life, which in turn, allows your relationships with friends and family to suffer, as you have difficulty finding balance in your life.

If you're not sure if you hold this trait, some questions you can ask yourself are:

- Do you find that you've sacrificed spending time with friends, family, and your partner because you had a project to do or you're staying late at work?

- Do your loved ones usually say, "You never spend time with us?"

- Does your boss ask you why you are always staying late at the office?

- Do people, such as your coworkers, tell you that there's more to life than work?

- Do you have difficulty juggling things in your life? For instance, is there always something in your life that gets neglected more than others?

- Do you still feel not enough or unworthy, regardless of all of the accomplishments and accolades you've received?

- Do you feel the people around you are better than you, so you try and push yourself more in order to measure up to them?

- Are you always beating yourself up when you don't complete a project quick enough?

- Do you feel shame or failure when you don't get a great mark at school, even though you worked extra hard on the task?

Chapter Two Soulwork

There are always going to be reasons you feel like an imposter in your own skin. Being aware of these character traits in yourself will help you see where you can improve your personal growth, so imposter syndrome becomes less and less a presence in your life. Something I want you to remember is this: One of the personality types we discussed can surely take precedence in your life, bringing fuel to imposter syndrome, or you can have a mix of these traits. I encourage you to give yourself grace and empathy as you start developing understanding and awareness of where imposter syndrome is showing up in your life.

For example, you may be a complete workaholic and try to be the superhero in your life and be a perfectionist at the same time. Boom, imposter syndrome! Or you might be a workaholic and neglect spending time with your friends and family because you are trying to do everything yourself. You wonder why the relationship with your partner is suffering, and you wonder why you're always feeling burned out and exhausted. When a co-worker tries to offer their help, you become upset and frustrated and feel like your whole world crashed down on you. You feel like no one thinks you're capable. It is so easy to struggle with imposter syndrome. Sometimes, you don't even know it's a part of you.

The first step to overcoming imposter syndrome is to understand how it presents itself in your life. Once you have an understanding, you'll have an idea of how to let it go. In order to help you increase your self-awareness, I've prepared a few journal prompts that you can answer to help you reflect. When you know where you stand, it'll feel easier to overcome feeling like an imposter every day. In order to help you increase your self-awareness, I've prepared a few journal prompts that you can answer to help you reflect. When you know where you stand, it'll feel easier to overcome feeling like an imposter every day.

1. Which imposter syndrome personality traits resonate with you the most? Why do you resonate with it?

2. How do you see these personality traits affecting your life choices personally and professionally?

3. What do you believe are some positive and negative emotions that tie your imposter

syndrome together? How do you see these personality traits affecting your personal and professional growth in the long run?

4. What do you need to do in order to let go of these personality traits, so they no longer affect your life?

In the next chapter, we'll be talking about finding a sense of calm before the storm takes over our lives. In other words, how to control our emotions and the importance of taking back control when we feel like we've lost our way. The next chapter is an important chapter, as therein, we will learn to navigate our emotions when feeling like an imposter. It will help you find a way to break through the barrier that felt impossible before. Now's your chance to ride the wave.

Chapter 3:

Finding Calm in the Storm

"The beauty of imposter syndrome is that you vacillate between extreme egomania and a complete feeling of: "I'm a fraud! Oh God, they're onto me. I'm a fraud!" So, you just try to ride the egomania when it comes and enjoy it, and then slide through the idea of fraud." –Tina Fey

The only thing we have control over is our emotions. We may feel like we are able to control external circumstances, such as what happens at our job or the arguments we have in our relationship; however, those situations are always out of our control. It doesn't matter if we do everything in our power to stay in control. The only thing that matters in the end is how we react to these situations.

This chapter is about understanding what areas our control is truly needed. Imposter syndrome can cause a tidal wave of chaos in our mind. It can play with our emotions so strongly that it feels like we'll never get over it, but I want you to know this: Even though it feels like you're so far down the rabbit hole of feeling like an imposter, despite your credentials, you can surely overcome it with flying colors.

This chapter is the start of showing you how.

What Is Control?

By definition, control means "to have direct influence over something or someone; or to have power or authority" (Merriam-Webster, n.d.).

So, many of us try our best to have control over every single thing that happens in our lives. By human nature, we dislike losing control over something. If we do, we feel like a failure. Because we feel that way, we try and do everything in our power to feel like a winner again. No one likes to feel like a failure, especially when we know we have extraordinary credentials under our belt, so we try to gain control over every circumstance, including the external ones. When we try to gain control, or in this case have influence over something, we tend to work harder than usual to try and prove ourselves to others. When it doesn't go the way we expect, our motivation is lost, and we feel unworthy or insufficient. Hello, imposter syndrome!

Our lack of control over external circumstances becomes such a sticky situation because we don't want to feel unworthy, but yet we are unable to change other people's opinion about us. We assume they see us as unworthy; however, it is only a presumption because we are not able to control what they think about us, and that makes us feel like we're doing something wrong, or we don't have enough knowledge to change their mind otherwise.

Wanting to have direct influence over something is a crazy vicious cycle in our lives that goes around and around like a Tilt-A-Whirl spinning out of control. If we keep at it, we'll never win and we'll never jump off that ride.

This may seem like a harsh statement–maybe it will trigger you–but there is truth in what I'm saying. The only thing that you can truly control in your life is your emotions. Consider it a blessing in disguise. You may not be able to control what people think of you, but you can certainly control the way you react to it. You may not be able to influence other people's validation towards you, but you can deeply influence how you treat yourself.

Internal Locus vs. External Locus

Lots of folks used the Covid-19 experience as a way to help them understand that, although many things happened during that experience, they learned about their own emotional control. People lost their jobs, businesses that have been around for many years got shut down, and depression and anxiety skyrocketed. No one knew what was going to happen; the only thing they were able to control is their emotional response to what was happening. Many used their job loss as an opportunity to create their own income and start their dream business. Others used the need for quarantine as an opportunity to spend time with their family and to connect with them on a deeper level. Everyone used this experience as a way to help them understand that, although they are unable to control what happens around them, they are able to control how they react.

We are reminded that we are always in control of our own destiny. No matter the situations we go through, it is up to us how we choose to respond.

Locus of control is the degree to which individuals perceive that outcomes result from their own behaviors or from forces that are external to themselves (mindtools.com, n.d.). In other words, the outcome of a situation is determined by one of two things: Your actions and behavior towards the result (internal locus of control), or how you believe the result is achieved based on what's happening around you (external locus of control).

Referring to the Covid-19 example, there were two different people that came out of it: The first group used the pandemic as a sign to create a more abundant life (internal locus), and the second group allowed the pandemic to shut them down emotionally, physically, and mentally, and they became depressed, burned out, and worried (external locus).

Imposter syndrome is the same. As a human, you have two choices: You can allow circumstances beyond your control to affect your success, or you can choose to react differently so that your success brings a more positive response. If you're allowing people to validate your worth and insinuate you're not good enough, your success (or lack thereof) will be determined by your belief. However, if you choose to believe that you are more than worthy and you have all the tools within you to create a successful life, the outcome will be different.

Understanding the Unknown

As you move forward, there is something you should always remember: You cannot control the unknown. You will never know what will happen before it happens. It is beyond our control; beyond our scope as humans. The only entity that truly knows the future is the universe. It knows the next steps you take or don't take. It is aware of the actions you take to achieve your goals, or the moments you procrastinate and feel like an imposter. There is no way for us to understand any of this. The only thing that is within our scope and knowledge is the way we react in the present moment.

But here's an extraordinary thing about what I just said. We may not be able to predict what happens in the future; however, the way we choose to react now can help shift its trajectory.

Most of us spend a lifetime trying to control the unknown, only to end up feeling defeated, unsuccessful, and undervalued. In these moments, imposter syndrome heavily sets in. Before you're deeper down the rabbit hole, I encourage you to shift your mindset and become aware of your emotional response to what is happening around you. For example, during experiences such as the Covid-19 pandemic, we are unable to control what happens around us, but we can choose to react to the situation in a way that we see it as a life lesson and a steppingstone for a greater life.

Losing Control in the Midst of Fear

When we feel like we are losing control, fear takes precedence in our life. We are not sure what's going to happen, so we feel scared. We feel uncertainty in the midst of controversial chaos, which ends up instilling anxiety, stress, and overwhelm in our body. When we are entrapped in uncertainty, we don't know what to do but feel scared. Our fear clouds our judgment, and we make decisions based on how scared and nervous we are rather than with confidence. When we make decisions based on this response, we later wonder why things are not going well and we start to question ourselves and our credentials.

It's not because we don't know what we are talking about—we have a wealth of skills and knowledge—but it's because we are allowing fear to control our beliefs and the decisions we make. This fear encourages imposter syndrome.

It is important to become aware of this as we go about our day. It's okay to not have the ability to control everything around you; there would be no life lessons if you had that much power. There would be no room for growth or inspiration, and you would run your life with ego instead of humility. Once you develop a full understanding that fear doesn't need to control your life, you'll accept the unknown with gratitude and peace. You won't feel like you're losing control, but instead, you'll feel confident, empathetic, and aligned.

When you feel like you're losing control, you can experience these symptoms:

- anxiety

- chronic stress

- depression

- lack of self-trust and confidence

- constant fear of unknown possibilities

- fear-based decisions

- sporadic, uncontrolled breathing

- anger, frustration and worry

- more bad days than good days

- feeling like you're being attacked and beat up by everyone

- lack of empathy and self-compassion

If this sounds like you, I encourage you to make a change. Understand that you're unable to control everything that happens around you. Understand that no matter what happens, you are going to be okay. Become aware of what is happening with your energy. Are you constantly living in fear, or are you okay with living with uncertainty and feeling certain about your emotions at the same time? You can choose to feel like your life is crashing down around you, or you can choose to understand the life lessons behind the struggle. What do they mean, and how can you regulate your emotions because of them?

Mastering Your Emotions

There are ways to regulate your emotions so that you don't feel like your world is crashing down around you and you're losing control. It takes a certain skill to understand yourself on a deeper level, but the great thing is that you are the only one that possesses this skill. No one can teach you how to master your emotions; sure, there are coaches and mentors out there that can offer you tips and advice, but ultimately, you are the only one that possesses the skill in order to master regulation effectively.

Before we get into some strategies and methods to help you through the journey, it is important we discuss some key skills for you to develop for your own personal growth.

Give Yourself Space

The worst thing we can do when we're trying to master our emotions is to ignore them. We don't know when we'll be angry or frustrated. It's kind of like a spur-of-the-moment situation. It can happen in an instant without notice. When certain emotions do show up, it is important you offer them the space they need to pass through your system.

If it's a negative emotion, learn to breathe through it until it softens, and you feel better. It is important that you don't get overworked and feel overwhelmed. It can become a ripple effect of negativity if it is uncontrolled. It is also important to slow down. When we feel angry, it feels like a bulldozer is just plowing through every poor victim in its wake. By giving yourself permission to slow down in the midst of anger, you're able to control your response and what happens moving forward.

Become Self-Aware

It is no secret that self-awareness is key when learning to regulate your emotions. Noticing how you feel can make or break the relationship with yourself. Take a moment to understand how you're feeling. If you're simply going about your day, trying to ignore your emotions, before you know it, they will heighten, and you will feel like you've lost control.

If you're feeling excited, notice how you feel in your body. Is your heart racing? Do you feel a tingling sensation in your fingers or your toes? Do you feel butterflies in your stomach? Are you having trouble sleeping because you're overly excited? Are you struggling with getting through your day because you can't wait for what's going to happen? Understanding your physical response to how you're feeling will help you become aware of how you usually respond when something exciting is coming your way.

As you're noticing your emotional symptoms in your body, it is important to also notice your physical symptoms. Do you feel sick because of how nervous you feel? Are you getting a migraine? Is your back or neck stiff and in pain? Are your muscles or joints aching? The way your body reacts to your emotions is usually a clear-cut sign that something is happening that your body may or may not like. It is important to pay attention to these symptoms so you can properly distinguish the strength of your emotions and then you can regulate them effectively instead of throwing spaghetti on the wall, hoping it will stick.

Name Your Emotion

You may notice that you're feeling emotional, but you may not understand exactly how you're feeling. For example, many people who feel depressed usually say the same statement: "I know I feel depressed, but I am not sure why." This is very common. It's okay to feel emotional, but if you're unsure how you're feeling, you won't know how to master it; therefore, you won't know how to heal from it.

A simple exercise you can do to help with this is to journal about it. In your journal, you can give your emotion a name. Begin your journal entry by using this journal prompt: *At the moment, I feel…* and then give it a name. Do you feel angry? Frustrated? Nervous?

Anxious? Resentment? Guilt? Shame? Judged? Criticized?

Once you are able to give it a name, you can give it a reason. *"I feel angry because of the fight I had with my partner." "I feel frustrated and annoyed because I didn't receive the promotion I thought I was going to get."* By giving your emotion a name, you are able to resonate with it on a deeper level and then go through the healing journey you need to go on.

You will learn more about how to name your emotion in chapter four; however, I thought I would give you a brief overview about what it entails here.

Acceptance

As humans, we dislike feeling negatively toward ourselves and others. We try to ignore our negative emotions and combat them immediately with a positive response as a way to deter us from feeling that way. However, by doing this, our negative emotions gain momentum until they feel difficult to control. In the midst of your emotions, it is important to accept and embrace them. It is important to remind yourself that you are only human and emotions, whether positive or negative, make you stronger and more determined.

By not allowing yourself to accept your negative emotions, it's as if you're not fully accepting yourself. By fully accepting the way you feel, regardless of the impact, you're able to heal and experience transformation. You're able to recognize that you're human and that the way you feel is valid.

Many of us have been told that it's not okay to have negative emotions. We've been told that when we feel that way, it is best to ignore and push them down and to try to be positive. That said, we're not robots. There are times where the situation calls for feeling negative and that's okay. The best thing you can do for your own mental and emotional health when that happens is to love yourself wholeheartedly and accept your emotions for what they are. It is important to give yourself grace and compassion at this moment, so you feel strong and unconditionally loved exactly as you are.

Live in the Moment

By practicing mindfulness, you're able to pay attention to your present surroundings. You're able to notice how you feel, the situations that trigger a negative response, and the messages your body gives you in order to tell you that something is wrong.

Mindfulness helps us engage in the present moment. If something is upsetting you, being mindful helps you understand why you're feeling that way and the best avenue to release your frustration. It is important to not give into any distractions that may deter you from your focus; pausing, taking a few deep breaths, and acknowledging your inner and outer surroundings will help keep your emotions intact.

Chapter Three Soulwork

Once you've begun to master your skills, you are able to strategize on how to get your emotions back on track, so the negative ones don't become the forefront of your emotional health.

This would be a great time to get out your journal and begin writing. Some questions you can yourself are:

- **Why am I feeling this way?** One of the most important things to remember is to not be afraid of your feelings. When we're afraid, we do everything in our power to ignore them, as we don't like feeling negatively; however, it is important to identify what's triggering you so you can acknowledge it and let it go.

- **What is my body trying to tell me?** Our physical symptoms matter. As we spoke about earlier, it is important to be mindful of how you're physically feeling. Pay attention to the way your body is reacting to your emotions. Are you feeling sick? Does your stomach ache? Do you feel pain in your lower back or neck? Does your head feel heavy?

- **What is the story I am currently telling myself?** When we experience a situation that throws us off course and distracts us in a negative way, we may create a negative belief in our mind. For example, if you didn't receive the promotion you were anticipating, you may feel it's because you're not smart enough or you don't have enough experience. If a date didn't go well or your relationship ended abruptly, you may tell yourself it's because you're not pretty enough. This belief will lead into another one that includes shame and guilt (I should've put in more effort.) Identifying the negative stories we're telling ourselves will not only help us acknowledge and accept our current beliefs, but it will help us create a new story as we heal.

- **Why am I telling myself this story?** How can I create a new one? Once you've identified your old limiting beliefs, you can accept them for their position in your life–they help you become more resilient and determined–and you can explore the reasons why you are telling yourself these stories. Maybe it's a cry for attention because you're feeling unloved. Perhaps it's a way to protect you from potential hurt. Going through self-discovery helps you understand how your mind thinks, which in turn, will help you master your emotions and identify them when something triggers you. When you're able to get a grasp of why these stories exist, you can begin to create a new story. One that is positive, passionate, and purposeful.

- **How will I respond?** When you're faced with a triggering situation, it is up to you how you choose to respond. You can respond with the same negative energy that it is bringing forth, or you can take a moment to breathe and respond in a softer tone. I encourage you to remember this quote by Tony Robbins when choosing to respond: "What you focus on, grows" (n.d.). If you choose to respond with negative energy, that's what you'll receive. However, if you opt for a positive and encouraging response, you'll receive the same energy in return.

The Covid-19 pandemic was a global lesson on control. We are unable to control the world, but we can control how we react to what happens. Once you master your emotions, you're able to take back control of your own life, where you are no longer run by fear, but you live your life in abundance and powerful self-leadership.

In the next chapter, we'll be discussing emotions in greater detail and the importance of naming your emotions so you can deeply understand where they're coming from and how to regulate them in a way where you have more control.

Chapter 4:

Naming Emotions

"Never be ashamed of what you feel. You have the right to feel any emotion that you want, and to do what makes you happy." –
Demi Lovato

It's no secret that we all have emotions. Some folks may be more in tune with their emotions than others—others may face challenges regulating emotions—and some have been taught and have learned to constantly hide their emotions and bottle them up. This learned behavior of bottling up emotions is usually rooted in fear. The fear that emotions are a weakness that could be used as leverage to be judged and taken advantage of.

No matter where you are with understanding your emotion, this chapter is a great opportunity to check in with yourself and expand your capacity for emotional intelligence (EQ). Emotional intelligence is "the capacity to be aware of, control, and express one's emotions, and to handle interpersonal relationships judiciously and empathetically" (Oxford dictionary, n.d.). We'll be discussing how to name your emotions so you can identify, acknowledge, and accept that they are a part of you. It is an important piece when it comes to overcoming imposter syndrome and learning to lean into your personal development.

It may not feel easy to name your emotions, especially if you have the belief system in place to ignore them until they pass, but let me assure you that this chapter will offer you some freedom and a potential breakthrough, especially in the midst of feeling like a fraud.

What Are Emotions?

I hope you're ready for a bit of a science lesson. We all have emotions, but have you ever given a thought as to what emotions are?

To put it in layman's terms, emotions are evolutionary triggers that help humans survive in a chaotic world. However, if you really wanted to get scientifically technical, the Berkeley Well Being Institute defines emotions as "biological states that come about as a result of thoughts, feelings and behaviors" (2011).

We are equipped with a set of predictable responses to situations. These responses can trigger basic emotions, such as anger, fear, happiness or joy, and sadness. The way you react to situations can trigger your mood and have physical effects on your body.

The Happiness Drugs

When you feel happy, your brain often releases four main chemicals. Some may refer to them as the *happiness drugs*: Endorphins, oxytocin, serotonin, and dopamine.

When you're happy, it becomes a vast ripple effect. You are in a positive mood, you have an extra bounce in your step, you laugh all the time, and the smallest things excite you. People love to be around your positive energy, and your entire day feels extraordinary.

The Not-So-Great Chemical

Now, what happens when you feel upset or frustrated? Your brain still releases a chemical, but instead, they're in the form of a negative energy called 'cortisol'. When cortisol is released into your system, it feels like a storm is washing away all of your happiness. You seem to be upset about everything, you frown, you cry, and nothing pleases you. People generally avoid this behavior, as they're afraid that something they say to you or the way they act could set you off. It still creates a ripple effect, but not a very good one. When you exhibit negative emotions, it feels as though nothing good is happening in your life and it feels as though there is no light at the end of the tunnel. Most often, you lose hope in the worst-case scenario.

You Are The Boss!

Here's something I want you to remember. Consider it to be excellent news. You have the power to control your emotions every day. You can stop your emotions from going sideways, where you feel like a toddler having an overexaggerated tantrum at the store because you didn't get what you wanted. Instead, you can opt to learn why you feel this way and name how you feel so it doesn't happen again. You are the boss of your emotions. You have the power to choose how and why they affect you.

If you are someone who struggles with controlling emotions on your own, please know that it's okay to get support. Support can come in the form of a coach, counselor, therapist, or support group. You are in charge, and it's up to you to build whatever supportive network you need.

Releasing the Chaos

Let's face it. Imposter syndrome can create a tidal wave of chaos in your mind. It virtually feels impossible to control when imposter syndrome takes over your mind, your actions and your body. In a way, imposter syndrome can present itself as an addiction. Many people can become addicted to drugs and alcohol; others can become addicted to failure and self-sabotage.

All this is doing is causing complete chaos in your mind and in your spirit. You think and believe things that are not true about yourself and about your accomplishments, the words you say to yourself sabotage you to the point of giving up regardless of how far you've come, and your emotions go haywire from negative to positive to negative again and again. It's like a tidal wave trying to wash away your journey every single day.

It is important to find a way to release the chaos from your mind. The chaos that is offering any feeble attempt to distract you from your goals. The chaos that feels like it's never-ending every day and keeps you up at night. The chaos that makes it feel like you're completely alone in the journey, no support to be found.

Does the chaos offer some kind of benefit?

To some degree, it does. Going through a difficult journey like this can help build your strength and resilience. It can help you understand that you have the courage within you to persevere; it's a matter of how far you are willing to go for your dreams.

On the other hand, if you're not mindful of how it's affecting your life, it can destroy your perseverance. It can destroy any hope you had of achieving your goals and any confidence you had of the skills and knowledge you embody. It is important to be mindful and painfully aware of how its negativity is decreasing your self-esteem and making you sabotage your every move.

The Emotion Wheel

The Emotion Wheel, also known as the 'Feelings Wheel', was created by psychologist Robert Plutchik. He created it as a representation of how our emotions work so that we are able to better understand our emotional state, from our inner world to our outer world.

By reflecting on the emotion wheel, we are able to grasp the potential results of what happens when our basic emotions grow stronger. Our basic emotions include anger, fear, sadness, joy, peace, and happiness.

The emotion wheel offers a variety of benefits:

- Learning about yourself on a deeper level by being able to name how you're feeling.

- Increasing empathy and compassion toward yourself and others.

- Emotional mastery.

- Better communication in terms of conflict resolution.

- Acknowledgement and acceptance of all your emotions.

If you feel like you're on an emotional rollercoaster, it will be helpful to use the emotion wheel as a guide to help you navigate them. You can pinpoint what the basic emotion is you're feeling and then dive deeper into regulating it with a stronger emotion that is affecting your confidence. Once you can name the emotions tied to your limiting beliefs, such as imposter syndrome, you'll be able to heal from them and develop a better understanding so you can release them for good.

Chapter Four Soulwork

Now that you have a better idea of how your emotional state works, it's time to put your knowledge into action. Make a commitment to yourself every day to write in your journal.

Write about your emotions. One journal prompt you can use is, "Today, I feel…" This is a simple, yet powerful, prompt that can begin a life-changing journey. You can learn so much about yourself using these three words.

Begin with a basic emotion and then dive deeper. Why do you feel that way? What situation is triggering you? What physical symptoms are you experiencing because of your feelings?

If it helps, I encourage you to use the emotion wheel to help pinpoint your deeper feelings. Begin with a basic emotion–do you feel fear, joy, peace, sadness, anger?– and then dive deeper. If you feel sad, find another term in the wheel that you relate to based on that basic emotion. This will help you develop an understanding of exactly how you feel and why you feel this way.

Writing about your emotional state will foster a deeper relationship with yourself, where you offer self-compassion and empathy. Free of judgment, you're able to be exactly who you are at the moment.

You now have a better idea of how to control your emotions when it comes to triggering situations. In the following chapter, we'll be discussing how to eliminate our limiting BS so we can live life in a positive way. It's not the BS you may be thinking of.

Keep on reading.

Chapter 5:

Eliminating Limiting BS

"I have spent my years at Princeton, while I was at law school and in my various professional jobs, not feeling completely a part of the worlds I inhabit. I am always looking over my shoulder wondering if I measure up." –Sonia Sotomayor

We all have limiting beliefs. Most of us developed them when we were children and we stepped into adulthood fully embodying and embracing these beliefs. Most of the time, these beliefs are on the subconscious level. We rarely have any awareness that they're a part of our lives and we go about our day with them being at the forefront of our existence.

One day we wonder why we keep procrastinating. We wonder why we never feel as though we are enough or worthy, and we wonder why we continue to stay exactly where we are, never moving forward. We become curious, and because of this curiosity, our consciousness begins to investigate the root of our beliefs so we can find a way to eliminate them.

This chapter is about exactly this. It's about learning how to eliminate the limiting BS in our lives. No, it's not the BS you're thinking of, although it is similar. Limiting BS, as in our limiting belief systems. The beliefs that affect our choices and the decisions that we make. The beliefs that keep us stagnant and feeling overwhelmed. The beliefs that give us a rollercoaster of emotions every single day. This is the BS I'm referring to.

We should know by now that imposter syndrome is one of our belief systems that we can choose to let go of. However, it's not the only one. What else is there? What other BS is currently controlling your choices and keeping you stuck feeling like an imposter? This chapter is going to help you become aware of all of it so you can understand why everything is around. Once you know, you can say goodbye for good.

What Are Belief Systems?

As humans, we are meant to adapt to the environment we are in. We learn to love, we find ways to fully accept ourselves, we fail, we win, we challenge ourselves, and we find ways to grow. While we do all this, we tend to also adopt certain belief systems. We create a set of beliefs throughout our life that determine right or wrong and true or false. As we grow up and learn to make our own decisions, these beliefs usually determine the success of our outcome. For example, we may grow up believing that financial abundance is not available to us; therefore, most decisions lead to a scarcity mindset. This mindset is what we're used to. It's how we were raised as children, watching our parents and elders struggle financially. As such, we adopt a belief that that's how we are supposed to live.

According to Psychology Today, "these shortcuts to interpreting and predicting our world often involve connecting dots and filling in gaps, making extrapolations and assumptions based on incomplete information and based on similarity to previously recognized patterns" (2018).

On another note, I would also like to mention that not all belief systems are bad. We can adopt many positive beliefs, which include abundance, happiness, joy, and prosperity. We can grow up living an extraordinary life full of freedom, where we were taught that we have the power to choose any type of life we desire to live. This becomes our set of beliefs, and we raise our family believing that freedom and abundance is meant for us, so we strive for it.

Your Belief Systems Can Impact Your Life

As you move forward in your life, I encourage you to remember this: Your belief systems can impact your life, creating positive or negative emotions within you that can either keep you stuck or motivate you toward your dreams.

Remember chapter four where we spoke about the importance of being mindful of our emotions? If we adopt negative beliefs, they can result in fear, worry, anxiety, and stress. These emotions can lead to depression, feeling like a constant failure, having an identity crisis, and losing sight of our goals and dreams. It is important to develop positive beliefs so you can move forward, knowing you are already successful, rather than stay stuck in overthinking mode because your negative beliefs are controlling your life. Chances are, you are the second person, otherwise you probably wouldn't be here reading a book about overcoming imposter syndrome. This chapter will offer you the tools that will help you reframe your mindset so you can stop digging a deeper hole.

To further explain this, I want to paint a little picture for you when it comes to positive and negative BS. Let's start with the negative.

Let's say your belief is that you don't have enough skills and knowledge to make it as a successful entrepreneur. You desire the freedom of working for yourself, but you feel stuck with the belief that you don't have what it takes. It doesn't matter if you have two university degrees under your belt plus a whole bunch of certifications; they are still not enough. You need more credentials, otherwise you'll never make it.

What happens when you feel this way? You are constantly worried, stressed, overwhelmed, burned out, panicked, and fearful of what could happen. Feeling inner peace is non-existent and survival mode is controlling your life. Excuses become the norm:

I need to get a job until I figure this out.

I need to enroll myself in another certification.

My degrees are not enough.

I need to acquire more knowledge somehow.

I don't have enough skills, otherwise I would've been successful already.

I'm too old to think this could work.

All my friends are successful; what do they have that I don't?

I'm running out of time. I need to do this now, otherwise it will be too late.

When these excuses show up, they become distractions. When they become distractions, you lose sight of your goal. When you lose your focus, the same negative emotions of worry, stress, and fear overtake you and you feel like you will never be successful.

The ripple effect of our negative BS becomes vast and controlling, so much so that we forget about being mindful and life becomes a blur. Hello, survival mode!

Now, for our positive BS.

You grew up with the belief that any form of success is available for you. You witnessed your parents have a strong and beautiful marriage (they still do), you watched your aunt and uncle grow a successful business that helped them travel all the time and buy your cousins anything they needed or wanted, your family's faith has always been strong and steadfast, and it seemed as though everyone you came across always felt peaceful and truly happy.

Because of this belief, you step into the world being mindful of your actions and believing that anything is possible. These beliefs result in stronger affirmations:

I can do this.

Everything is possible.

I have all that I need within me to make things happen.

I can create any type of freedom and success that I want.

I know what I want, and I will do everything in my power to get it.

I am already living an abundant life.

These beliefs translate into feeling unconditionally loved and guided by the universe, self-trust, compassion, empathy, strength, resiliency, determination, peace, commitment, motivation, and happiness. When you're feeling this way, nothing can stop you. You use challenges as fuel to motivate and inspire you to become a greater version of yourself. You achieve your own version of success because you desire to, not because someone told you need to. You make your mark in the world not because you are chasing success, but because you believe you are already successful no matter what.

See the difference between the negative and positive BS?

Your belief systems will impact your life in the way that you choose they will. If you choose to believe in the positive, you will strive. If you choose to believe in the negative, you will feel stuck.

That being said, I want you to remember something. Even if you grew up embracing negative beliefs, it is never too late to reframe your mindset. You have the power to choose differently. To be different. To change the old negative stories you grew up with into positive ones. One of the beautiful things about this choice is that no one can make it for you but you.

Ask yourself: What am I choosing today?

Reframing Your Mindset

There are a few things you can do to help reframe your mindset from negative BS. It will take some work and a bit of patience, commitment, and dedication to healing, but it's not impossible.

- **Self-accountability.** It is important to remain in integrity with yourself and your goals. When you don't hold yourself accountable, you lose your focus and then you find yourself deeper down the rabbit hole. Reframing your mindset is not an easy task, but it is also not impossible. It requires you to come back to your inner truth to ask yourself why you desire to make the change; once you know, you'll stay motivated.

- **Understanding what is true and what is false.** Just because you believe something, doesn't mean it's the truth. It could be a false belief that you created for yourself years ago, or a belief someone told you because it was what they believed, so you believed it to be true. Understanding whether the belief is true or false will help you reframe your mindset in a positive way. You can choose whether the belief is either true or false. For example, do you truly believe that you'll never find a great relationship, or will you choose to believe that the right partner is out there for you? Do you choose to believe that you will constantly struggle financially, or do you choose to believe that you are always surrounded by abundance, and it is available for you?

- **Consistency is key.** As with all things, putting your reframe on repeat is important. If you want to have a dream body, you can't just workout once and receive it. It takes consistency and dedication every day with eating healthy food and staying active. Reframing your mindset is the same. It doesn't work if you say the affirmation only once. It requires you to consistently motivate yourself and hold yourself accountable for changing your beliefs. Once you choose new beliefs, repeating them constantly to yourself will further affect the change and impact your results.

Tools for Reframing Your Beliefs

In order to help you in your journey, there are a few tools you can use as you practice awareness and accountability. These tools are known to help greatly when reframing your mindset for positivity.

- **Acknowledge and accept the negative BS.** Write each of these beliefs down in your journal and discuss them with yourself. Have a deeper understanding as to why they showed up in the first place. Is it because your parents shared this belief with you, and you believed it to be true since then? How has it made you feel? How is it currently controlling your decision-making? How has it affected your life? Once you are aware of its power, you're able to accept the belief for what it is and then reframe it into a positive. The negative BS could be, *"I will never be successful,"* and the positive reframe can shift to, *"I am experiencing success every single day."*

- **Create a list of the negative BS and express gratitude.** Be thankful for every single belief on this list. Give thanks that it showed up when it did because it challenged you and helped you become resilient. I also encourage you to show yourself empathy because of this list. Read each one and forgive yourself for believing it when it wasn't true. Beside every negative BS, counteract it with a positive BS just as we did in the first point. This tool is a powerful one because you are not only acknowledging the limiting belief, but you are rewiring your subconscious mind, so it creates a new story.

- **Practice mindfulness.** It is important to be mindful when it comes to your belief systems. This will help you gain a deeper understanding of how they are currently impacting your life. Once you develop self-awareness, when the belief shows up, you can reframe it immediately and discredit its negativity.

Chapter Five Soulwork

The only way reframing your mindset will work is if you take consistent, intentional action. Without inspired action, your beliefs will stay the same.

Your journal prompts for this chapter are:

- What am I choosing today? What beliefs do I currently have? Are they true or false?

- If I choose the negative BS, how is it currently impacting my life? What would happen if I chose positive BS? How will my life change?

By answering these questions, you are honoring the relationship with yourself on a deeper level. I encourage you to ask yourself these questions every single day. The answer will determine how greatly your life is impacted in either a positive or negative manner.

This chapter is a beautiful segue into the following chapter. It will be discussing what can happen if you choose to stay in a stuck and stagnant mindset instead of desiring to move forward with your goals and dreams. It will give you an idea of how your life can change, almost instantly in fact, if you choose to make this change.

Chapter 6:

Fixed Mindset Versus Growth Mindset

"Growth is an uncomfortable process. Think about a seed that has been sowed. In order for the seed to bloom into a plant, it must first split in half, borrow downward with roots, and push upward toward the sun. Nothing about that is easy, but nevertheless, it's possible." –Sydney Jackson-Clockston

Every single day, we can choose to grow in our personal and professional development, or we can choose to stay the same. If we stay the same, we disregard the life lessons that come with learning about ourselves, and we create a negative impact moving forward. If we choose growth, we learn many inexplicable things about ourselves and our relationship to life.

This chapter is about helping you go from feeling stagnant and never moving forward to creating a deeper relationship with yourself, where your mess (old stories, negative BS) becomes your message (positive BS, abundance, transformation).

What Is a Fixed Mindset?

I want to paint you a clear visualization of what happens when you stay in a fixed mindset.

It is important to continue growing, even if you cannot physically witness your growth yet. Imagine a beautiful seed that is being planted on the earth. You dig up the soil so it's deep enough, place the seed in the hole, cover it up, and then you wait. Every single time you nurture and water the seed, the plant is growing. You can't see what's happening underneath the surface; you can only trust that growth is occurring. By faith, you believe it is. You don't leave it to grow by itself; you continue to water it and take care of the seed. Without love, care, and proper nutrients, the growth of the seed is non-existent. Before you know it, a leaf starts to sprout from beneath the ground. Something is happening. Growth is happening. Evolution is occurring. As you continue to care for the plant, it grows bigger, brighter, and more beautiful, until it blooms into a magnificent flower.

I want you to think about something. What do you feel would happen if you stopped caring for the flower when it blooms? What would happen if you stopped nurturing it and giving it water? More than likely, it will dry up and die, and you'll need to start over with another seed and go through the same process.

So many of us are prone to staying in a fixed mindset. We achieve our goals and then we stay there. We no longer have any interest in nurturing our goals that, years down the road, we are in the exact same place as we were several years before that. We've lost our passion and commitment and we've become comfortable.

When you stay in a fixed mindset, many negative emotions can show up—worry because you're not sure where to go next, stress because everything feels like a routine, boredom because everything feels the same with no excitement, and fear because you have no idea what's going to happen a year from now. In a fixed mindset, there is no projection, and when there's no projection, innovation doesn't exist. When you don't find ways to grow, you stay stuck. When you feel stuck, you overthink. When you overthink, you lose your passion and sight of your purpose. It becomes a downward spiral of conflicting emotions because you're not sure of what to do or who to be anymore. It's like you've lost yourself.

What Is a Growth Mindset?

Now that you have an idea of what happens when you stay in a fixed mindset, I'd like to explain what happens when you choose to continually grow.

I'd like to use another powerful visualization in order to help explain the growth mindset.

I believe that butterflies are one of the most beautiful insects. My home state of Colorado is right in the migration path of Monarch butterflies. Almost every fall, it's possible to witness swarms of monarchs in the gardens, parks, and open fields. Each monarch has its own unique quality that makes them as beautiful as they are. At times, we tend to forget the journey a butterfly has to go through in order to be viewed as extraordinary.

The transformation is called metamorphosis. It includes four stages of growth: The egg, caterpillar, transition, and re-birth. Each and every stage has its own mess that turns into a beautiful transformation. The female butterfly lays her eggs, which hatch into caterpillars. The caterpillar's job is to continually eat as much as it can, and as it grows, it sheds layers multiple times. It's as if it's letting go of its old self so it can be replaced with a new version. Once the caterpillar grows into the appropriate size, it doesn't stop the growth completely. It moves onto the next stage. The transition. The innovation. It transforms into a chrysalis and goes through a re-birth journey. The caterpillar is known to die in the chrysalis and begin to take shape as a butterfly. It can take a few weeks or months—only time will tell—but once it's ready, it emerges from the chrysalis as a beautiful flying insect.

A butterfly's journey is an extraordinary representation of growth. We may not know what's happening inside the chrysalis, but a transformation is taking shape. As a caterpillar, it goes through various struggles, fighting off bigger insects, struggling with trying to survive through weather changes, and finding enough food to eat so it can continue to grow and survive, but it never quits. The caterpillar doesn't stay exactly as it is; it does whatever it can to survive so it can innovate and move onto the next stage of becoming a butterfly, despite the mess it takes for it to get there.

We can certainly learn about our own personal development by reminding ourselves of a butterfly's journey. Developing a growth mindset is about moving forward, no matter the struggles we go through. Many of us stay in a fixed mindset because we go through a situation that is difficult to overcome and we feel we can't move past it. These are the icky limiting beliefs we spoke about in chapter five. By choosing to remember that these situations are helping us become stronger and more resilient to challenges, we can continue to innovate and go through our own rebirth and come out on the other end as a strong-willed and determined butterfly.

What Happens Next?

It is important to remember to give yourself time. Give yourself the space you need to transition and transform. While in the fixed mindset, use it as an opportunity to slow down, understand, and learn about yourself. Everyone makes mistakes; we are human. Practice self-reflection to understand our life lessons. This important process will help you step into a growth mindset. Be patient with yourself and the journey– trying to rush the process is a setup for failure and will only allow your limiting beliefs to creep back in, keeping you stuck at square one.

A few ways that can also help as you transition from a fixed to a growth mindset are:

Affirmations

Affirmations are powerful statements for growth. They help you have a deeper connection to yourself so you can learn to love yourself unconditionally. I would like to offer a full disclaimer, though: Not all affirmations will work with your transformation. There are many positive statements you can say to yourself to help instill growth and self-love. I encourage you to find affirmations that relate to you and your journey. Find statements that speak to you and make you happy. Those are the ones that will be more effective. If you're unable to find ones that resonate with you, I suggest you create your own. Be creative and create them with your growth in mind.

Choosing Your Focus

When wanting to step into a growth mindset, it is important to be wary of where your focus goes. Associating yourself with negative people will simply keep you in a fixed, negative mindset. The great Nipsey Hussle said, "If you look at the people in your circle and don't get inspired, then you don't have a circle. You have a cage" (n.d.) If you desire growth, start hanging with people who have the same mentality and find mentors to help support your journey. Same goes with the social media content you consume. Reading news articles every day and being distracted by random

Instagram reels will keep you in a fixed mindset, where you are constantly living in fear, worry, and stress. I encourage you to be mindful of what you view on social media. Ask yourself how it will help you with your growth. If you come to the conclusion that it doesn't, have the strength to shut it off and move on.

Mindfulness

Being mindful is about becoming aware of what you do on a daily basis. Are you doing it intentionally or without purpose? Do you notice you're spending a lot of time on social media and getting distracted by playing your games instead of working on the projects you're excited to work on? What are the words you are saying to yourself? They matter more than you may realize. Are they words of hope, inspiration, and encouragement? Or are they words that consist of shame, guilt and failure? Are you getting enough rest, or are you working until you can't keep your eyes open any longer? Mindfulness is incredibly important for your personal and professional growth. What you do and who you are in your present will determine how far you grow.

Chapter Six Soulwork

Going from a fixed mindset to a growth mindset takes a lot of work, dedication, and consistency. With time, you will experience the changes. I like to compare it to going to the gym. You don't see gains (growth) by visiting one or two times. To get any results, consistency is key.

The following exercise will help the transition feel smoother and more effective:

In your journal, write down a mistake you have made in the past. It could be anything–a mistake you made while learning something new, maybe you misunderstood the instructions for a task at work and did it incorrectly, maybe a social faux pas where you said something you wish you hadn't, or you snapped at someone and regretted it later. You felt shame and you somehow wished you could take it back.

As you reflect on this situation, write down and answer the following questions:

- What happened? Write down the facts in detail as if it's an outsider looking in.

- What were the consequences?

- Did you have the opportunity to correct the mistake? If so, what was the result? How did it make you feel?

Now, make two columns:
- On the left side, write what you remember saying to yourself about the mistake. Think about what you said both immediately, afterward, and later on. Try to be as honest as

possible and give as many phrases as you can recall or that you might say in a similar situation. Ask yourself the same questions as you did in the beginning:

- ○ What were the consequences?
- ○ Did you have the opportunity to correct the mistake? If so, what was the result? How did it make you feel?

- On the right side, reflect on how you can reframe your statements (the words you said to yourself in the left column). How can you reframe your self-talk so that it is forgiving of your mistake and reflects a growth mindset? What have you learned about this experience?

As you step into a growth mindset and shed your layers of a fixed one, it's time to find your own success. The following chapter will demonstrate how to redefine your own success rather than 'keep up with the Jones".

Chapter 7:

Redefining Success

"Be thankful for what you have; you'll end up having more. If you concentrate on what you don't have, you will never, ever have enough." –Oprah Winfrey

The previous quote may feel cliche, but I want you to ask yourself these questions:

What does success mean to you? How do you define success?

They may seem like the questions mean the same, but in truth, they are different. You may feel that success means having your dream home, lots of money in your bank account, living on the beach, and traveling the world, but you could define success as freedom, abundance, overcoming challenges, and creating phenomenal experiences that take your breath away.

This chapter is about helping you create fulfillment in your life. First, defining what it means to experience fulfillment; and second, using that definition to create your own version of success.

Your definition could mean a variety of different things as you go through life and experience a different journey. That's what is important about not staying in a fixed mindset as we spoke about in the previous chapter. If you keep yourself in a fixed mindset, your version of success will always stay the same; if you're okay with that, then all the power to you. However, if you're anything like me, I would much rather innovate my definition of success as I continue to reach new levels of myself.

This chapter will help you learn:

- Why it's important to create your own version of success rather than copy someone else.

- Why 'keeping up with the Jones' is not a great strategy.

- The importance of believing in your own success, even when others say it's impossible. It may feel like a lonely journey at times, but it is definitely worth it.

- How to have a sense of fulfillment and purpose in everything you do.

Defining Success as You Grow Up

What do you want to do when you grow up? Who do you want to be?

As children, it is common for our parents to ask us these questions. It never fails, especially when we are just about to graduate from high school. Many kids say things like, "I want to be an astronaut, fireman, policeman, or the President of the United States," or if you're in my family, you have people like my brother, who says, "I want to be a duck when I grow up." Yes, a duck. He said this when he was only six years old. At this age, being a duck felt so exciting. Of course, my family did not protest or tell him that he couldn't be a duck as an adult. We never told him that it was an impossible dream. We wanted him to dream and have a creative imagination, and that he did. We also knew that the world would snap him back into reality and squish his imagination, but he needed to find that out for himself rather than oppose negative beliefs unto him and grow up thinking that achieving his dreams wasn't possible.

A similar situation happens to most of us. As children, we become so good at dreaming and dreaming BIG. We watch a bunch of cartoons on Saturday and Sunday mornings that help us have a creative imagination. All of a sudden, we envision ourselves being a mermaid or riding a unicorn along a rainbow road. We dream of having ice cream and cookies until we get sick, and we believe that this is the life to have. We allow ourselves to believe in any and ALL possibilities, no matter what it looks like or how crazy it is. As kids, we never believed that our dreams were impossible or crazy until we met someone that told us they are. In a blink of an eye, the balloon that we were flying high on with our imagination popped and we began to descend from the clouds. Our dreams, the possibilities are crushed and trampled on just like that. As we grow older, we meet people that tell us what we can and cannot do. And we begin to believe it ourselves. We lose all hope that our dreams are possible because someone told us that it's hopeless. Then Boom! We find ourselves stuck, lost, feeling like an imposter and failure, trying to find a new dream in hopes that we finally experience fulfillment.

The way I see it, this is all part of the journey. We learn about our strength and resilience in these moments. We learn about how to overcome challenges when they're presented to us and to remain focused on achieving our dreams, despite the Negative Nellies in our life. As we grow up, we discover who's feeding into our fixed mindset and who's encouraging and inspiring our growth. Awareness becomes imminent in our lives, and when we're ready to reframe our story, we begin to define and create our own version of success.

External Success Versus Internal Success

When I thought about what success means to me, I always thought about materialized possessions: An overflow of money, a big, gigantic house, and a beautiful car that everyone can be envious of. For a long time, I believed that having all of these things meant that I am successful. It meant that I truly *made it in my life,* and everyone can be proud of what I've accomplished.

But as I went through my own personal development journey, I realized that this was not true success for me. I discovered that authentic success was keeping in alignment with my inner truth, and who I am on a deeper level was worth way more than materialistic gold. I already carried gold within me; that felt more than enough for me. It made me happy, fulfilled, and successful, despite not having any of the materialism.

This is the difference between external success and internal success. External success is about 'keeping up with the Jones" and remaining in competition about who's more successful. The more you have, the more successful you are. This will only make you happy temporarily. Internal success is about determining success on your terms. Finding out what makes you excited and lit up. Discovering what you're meant to do in this world and doing it with passion, courage, and purpose. Feeling at peace with what you have and being okay with living without what you don't have.

I believe there's a bit of a flaw with society's way of living. Everyone expects you to live, breathe and dress a certain way. They expect you to have certain things and if you don't have them, you're not worth their time. To me, that's flawed. We can certainly find authentic fulfillment and success without having to compete in a materialistic world. You don't need to have a lot of money in your bank account to feel successful. You can have $10 and still feel incredibly abundant. You don't need to have a fancy car in order to feel fulfilled. You can have an old beater that gets you from point A to point B and still feel like the happiest person on the planet.

I encourage you to remember all of this as you move forward in your life. It's great to have the materialistic stuff, but it does not and will not determine your worth and value in this world. You determine your value, and you determine how successful you choose to become, with or without these things.

Copying Others' Success Is Not a Great Strategy—Here's Why

Here's the thing about trying to make others' success your own. There is no fulfillment in doing it this way. You may experience fulfillment in the beginning, feeling like things are working in your favor, but eventually, you come to terms with their success not feeling authentic to you. When you get to this point, imposter syndrome becomes stronger. You think: *What am I doing wrong? Why am I not as successful as them? I'm doing everything they're doing–what's wrong with me? Why doesn't it feel the same? What else do I need to learn in order to achieve the same success?* It's a downward ripple effect of unanswered questions, worry, stress, fear, and anxiety.

I've seen it time and time again with many people in business, especially online coaches who are starting out. They follow and study every move of a successful coach in their industry. When it's time to take action, they attempt to copy the idea of a successful program this coach offers. *If this program is successful for them, it should work for me too.* They create a similar version, launch it, and they wonder why it failed. They feel that they didn't study the coach's strategy and delivery as much as they should have, so they enroll themselves into their program again to try and figure out what they missed. And boom! Epic fail. Again. These new coaches are left scratching their heads and wondering what's wrong with them.

This story may relate to you, and if it does, I want you to know something. There is absolutely nothing wrong with you. You are simply not meant to copy your mentors. You're meant to find your own way and discover your own unique method. In chapter six, I spoke about choosing your focus. If you're following others that make you feel intimidated, an imposter, and inferior to them because you haven't quite got it yet like they have, I encourage you to find another tribe. Copying others because they already have success is never a great strategy for your own personal and professional development. This is never a way to help you define your own success. All this will do is help you feel like more of an imposter and failure than ever. Find a way to crawl out of the rabbit hole where you're no longer copying others because they're inspiring, but rather, you're making your own unique mark in the world.

Defining Success Now

As you move forward with your goals, it is important that you know why you wish to accomplish them. Without a reason, it's as if you're throwing spaghetti to the wall hoping that it sticks. And if it doesn't, you're somehow okay with it. That doesn't feel like success to me.

When you know where you're going and why you want to get there, it'll feel easy to motivate and inspire yourself.

There are several questions that you can ask yourself that will help you create your own definition of success:

- Do I define success as having wealth?

- Do I define success as having a ton of wisdom?

- Do I define success as having unconditional self-love and confidence?

- Do I define success as being mindful and aware of my surroundings?

- Do I define success as having many employment opportunities knocking at my door?

- Do I define success as showing compassion for others and helping and supporting others who are less fortunate?

- Do I define success as creating harmony and balance in my life?

- Do I define success as a new job promotion?

- Do I define success as spending every evening with my family having dinner?

- Do I define success as achieving every dream on my vision board?

- Do I define success as being able to travel anywhere in the world?

- Do I define success as living on the beach and swimming in the ocean every day?

- Do I define success as receiving a paycheck every two weeks?

- Do I define success as having the freedom to live on my own terms and create my own economy?

- Do I define success as being able to pay for my children's college degrees without the aid of student loans?

- Do I define success as being in integrity with my own boundaries when I experience difficult clients?

- Do I define success based on the people I choose to surround myself with?

- Do I define success as knowing what my purpose is and striving to fulfill it?

- Do I define success as overcoming challenges that I didn't think I would surpass?

- Do I define success as finding a way to believe in myself when no one else did?

- Do I define success as becoming authentic and true to myself as much as I possibly can?

All of these questions have the power to start you off on the right foot when it comes to creating your own freedom. The answers to these questions can help you define success in a way that is unique and authentic to you, without feeling the need to copy others or see others as competition. By answering these questions truthfully and with integrity, you're able to understand what you value most in this world without feeling like you need to prove yourself to others to be successful.

The Importance of Believing in You

There is no doubt that the road to success can be a lonely one, especially if you have a lot of Negative Nellies in your life that try to steer you off course and distract you as much as they can. It will feel like no one believes in you and what you have to offer. You may even question whether creating your own definition of success is worth it.

I want you to know something if you're in this boat. It's pretty simple–as long as you believe that you can achieve your dreams and be successful, the journey would always be worth it. It shouldn't matter if your friends and family don't believe your dreams are possible. They're not living them; you are. They're not going through the work, the healing, or the transformation; you are. Yes, they will be affected indirectly, especially when you become successful, but your dreams will only come into fruition if you choose to put in the effort. Your own version of success will only happen if you set your mind to create it. That's the beautiful thing about creating our own success. No one can do it for us. It's up to us to spur into inspired action with our dreams at the forefront of our success.

I understand how it may feel hard to believe in yourself when it seems like no one believes in you. This is why self-confidence and trust are so important, especially when our success is at the root of it.

There have been many instances where I've heard of people telling their friends and family to get a real job and to stop thinking about becoming an entrepreneur. If every single person followed this advice and allowed other's limiting beliefs to affect them, there wouldn't be many people in this world changing lives and helping others. They would listen to their people and find a mediocre job they weren't happy with and try to find a sense of fulfillment somehow. Instead, they chose to listen to their heart and step up to become a higher version of themselves who experiences success and fulfillment on their own terms.

This is my hope for you. That you choose to create your own version of success, despite the negativity around you. That you choose to move along your own unique path, creating success in a way that lights you up every single day. That you choose to be, do, and have any success you desire because it is what your heart is longing for and it is what excites you, rather than go after the success people tell you're capable of.

Chapter Seven Soulwork

I encourage you to reflect on your definition of success so you can strive forward, rather than take a few steps back.

In your journal, reflect on the following:

- The questions in **Defining Success Now.** Answer them truthfully. Even though they are "yes" and "no" questions, dive deeper and truly go through a reflection journey. You might surprise yourself with your answers if you learn to come into accordance with your authenticity and unique way of life.

- What do you see as fulfillment and purpose in your life? What does this mean to you?

- How did you define success five years ago? How do you define it now? Answering these questions may offer you a breakthrough, as the answers will demonstrate how much you've changed since then, or it may offer you an inner truth that you're still in a fixed mindset. By holding yourself accountable, you can understand what you still need to learn about yourself and your choices.

As you reflect on this soulwork, you may come across other questions you can ask yourself when it comes to your success. Just go with it. Go with the flow and see what happens. There are no right or wrong answers when it comes to defining what success means for you. The definition is unique to you and you alone. Trust the process and see what you come up with.

As we dive into the last chapter, remember what success and fulfillment looks like for you. Chapter nine is about setting smart goals—a perfect segue from a chapter that spoke about redefining success.

Keep your definition in mind as you move forward with the last piece of this book.

Chapter 8:

Setting Smart Goals

"The only impossible journey is the one you never begin." –Tony Robbins

To begin this chapter, I want you to visualize with me again.

Imagine you are at a gas station. It's late at night, your car is nearing the empty signal on your gas tank, so you need to stop for gas. You don't see a gas station for miles, but finally, you find one. As your tank is filling, you take out your map. You have an idea of where you are, you know where you need to go, and your map will help guide you in the right direction. You pull out of the gas station, and even though it's late and it's a bit too dark to see the road signs, your map is your guide, the key to getting to your destination safely.

You know what success means for you—you've defined it in the previous chapter—and you know where you want to go, so you need to set goals in order to achieve fulfillment. Not just any goals; smart, clearly defined goals that get you motivated and inspired to keep going.

This chapter is about helping you create these goals. It's about helping you create a unique plan that strategizes the best way to reach your goals. We always make many goals: We strive to quit smoking, increase our monthly income, eat healthier, go to the gym five times per week, find a well-paying job, and start a business. That said, sometimes we lack the motivation to achieve these goals. I see it especially as the New Year comes around the corner. Everybody always has New Year's Resolutions. The new year is upon us, and everyone is so excited to achieve their goals by the following new year. By the time we are only a few months into the year, we have all forgotten about our goals.

Why?

- life gets in the way
- we become distracted with survival mode
- we lack motivation
- we're not inspired enough
- the goals are not clearly defined. There is no staying power

Because of these reasons, our goals go down the drain with us feeling guilty, ashamed, and unmotivated because we couldn't achieve a simple task we desired to do that would better our lives.

This chapter is about helping you get out of that funk of not achieving your goals. Now that you know how to define your success, it's time to create a plan to help you get there. It is my hope with this chapter that you feel inspired to achieve your goals, no matter the challenges, obstacles, or excuses you come across. By setting smart goals for your life, you can have more clarity, direction, and purpose when aligning yourself to the direction of your dreams.

What Are SMART Goals?

I am sure you have an idea of what your goals are, but are they *smart* goals? Do they have a clearly defined action plan? Do they feel impossible to reach? Can you wrap your head around the results of these goals?

These are questions you can ask yourself in order to determine if your goals are smart goals or not.

SMART is an acronym for the following:

Specific

Measurable

Achievable

Relevant

Time Bound

Bill Copeland, an American author, says this: "The trouble with not having a goal is that you can spend your life running up and down the field and never score" (n.d.).

We all love the idea of having goals, but if our motivation isn't inspiring enough, we lack the passion to achieve our goals. We run around with our heads cut off like chickens, pretending to be inspired, but in reality, we wish we could achieve our goals without having to do anything. We lack the inspired action that sets our bum on fire.

Creating goals using the SMART acronym will help you keep your motivation. It defines your reasons for creating your goals, it helps you define measurable action steps that feel achievable, and it helps you set specific goals, so you know exactly where you want to go.

How Do You Create SMART Goals?

Let's break it down.

- Be **Specific**. In order to know the right path to take on your map, your goals need to be as specific as possible. It is also important that your goals are simple, concise, and unique to you. If they're not, your goals may feel like they're hard to achieve, and you won't feel motivated to achieve them. You can ask yourself some questions that will help you uncover some details about your goals:

    o Why is it important for me to achieve my goals?

- What do I hope to get out of achieving my goals?
- What would happen if I didn't achieve my goals?
- What is stopping me from achieving my goals? What are my limiting beliefs, and how can I reframe them?

- Have **Measurable** Goals. In order to track the success of your goals, you need to be able to track your progress. Tracking your progress consistently will remind you how much further you need to go to reach your destination, and it will keep you accountable, so you don't miss your mark. When you reach your goals, you'll be able to celebrate your progress and you'll have an idea of the next steps you need to take. Some questions you can reflect on in order to understand if your goals are measurable are:

  - How long will it take me to achieve my goals?
  - How many goals do I currently have? What are they?
  - How much time do I need to spend taking action every day?
  - How will I know if I've hit a milestone?

- How will I know if my goals have been achieved?

- Are My Goals **Achievable**? In order to reach your goals successfully, they need to feel like they're possible but, at the same time, challenge you to grow on a deeper level. Many people's goals are realistic, but they're not challenging enough, so they get bored and move on. Achievable goals will stretch you to a greater version of you while keeping your head out of the clouds, feeling like they're impossible. A couple questions you can ask yourself are:

  - How achievable are my goals? Do I believe they're possible? If you believe you can achieve them, then you will.

  - How realistic is the outcome of my goal? For example, you can't shoot for $10,000 per month in your business when you haven't made a cent yet. Shoot high, but still be as realistic as possible so you don't freak out and, all of a sudden, lose your motivation because your goals are too high. Instead, maybe opt for setting a goal of $500 per month and then increase it as your confidence increases.

- Have **Relevant** Goals. It is important that your goals resonate with you and align with the other goals you have. If you don't feel the sense of urgency of your goals, you won't feel inspired to achieve them. By creating relevance, you take back control of your goals and the action steps needed to get there. To help determine the relevance, ask yourself these questions:

    o Are my goals connected to my why?

    o Do my goals align to my current lifestyle and other goals?

    o Is it the right time to strive for my goals?

    o What happens if I don't feel the sense of urgency with my goals? What do I need to do? How do I need to shift my mindset?

- Set a **Time**. With any goal, they require a deadline. If there's no deadline, you won't know how much time you have left to complete your goals; therefore, you'll have the option to change it and not hold yourself accountable for completing it. Your goal is not measurable; as such, it won't feel achievable, and you will refrain from holding yourself responsible for not accomplishing your goals. You blame it on life's distractions, the busyness of your business, your side hustle, part-time job, or family engagements. When you set a deadline for accomplishing your goal, it's as if you set a verbal contract with yourself. In the back of your mind, you know you're closer to your deadline every single day; therefore, you do everything in your power to achieve it by then. Some questions you can ask yourself that will help keep you accountable are:

- What do I need to do today in order to take action?

- What is the result of accomplishing my goals six months from now?

- What are the results one year from today?

Potential Obstacles and Solutions

Although setting SMART goals is quite effective and helps you become clear, focused, and driven in accomplishing your goals, there are also a few potential pros and cons that can occur while setting specific goals. To be honest, no one likes to think of the cons, as they are negative pieces of our journey, but it's important to be aware of both sides of the story so you can make decisions efficiently. Understanding them also sets you up for success instead of allowing you to only think of the positives and feel like a failure because you weren't aware of potential challenges and obstacles.

The Cons

- **You can get very addicted to achievement.** While goal-setting is important in order to make the life of our dreams a reality, we need to be careful when setting specific goals, especially when we reach them. When we achieve our goals, we get excited and celebrate, and that alone can become an addiction. We may neglect our family and special events, going out with friends, forgetting about taking care of ourselves, because all we want to do is achieve our goals. While that seems fine, it is important you acknowledge your life outside of goal-setting as well so that it doesn't become an obsession.

- **You try to do things yourself.** When we accomplish our goals, at times, we may think we achieved them by ourselves, without any help from our team or spiritual guides. We neglect that we had help from the universe or from a team that also put in hard work. When this happens, our ego and pride get in the way, and we neglect our faith; therefore, it is important to be mindful and express gratitude to the universe and our physical team regularly for partnering with us to accomplish our goals.

- **Fear of failure.** When it comes to goal-setting, fearing failure can be a big challenge, especially when we don't achieve our goals by the deadline. If we don't, stress, worry, and fear get in the way and begins to control our decision-making. For some of us, we may take it hard when we don't accomplish our goals. It is important to remember to keep going when the goals you set don't come into fruition when you expect them to. It may be because of uncontrollable factors, or it may be because it wasn't the right time for them to happen. Don't allow this setback to skyrocket negative emotions, where you end up quitting. Keep going, no matter what.

- **Setting your goals based on other's goals.** To put it simply, goal-setting isn't a marathon. Just because your friend set their goal to buy their dream house in a few months does not mean you need to beat yourself up and feel shame when it hasn't happened to you yet. Goal-setting is individual and based on unique circumstances. What I've learned about effective goal-setting is to be realistic and not rush the process. Take your time and enjoy the journey. When it's meant to happen for you, it will happen.

- **Making unrealistic goals.** So many of us become overly ambitious when it comes to goal-setting. We set a goal of making $10,000 per month when we haven't even made $1000. It is important to set strong, realistic goals that you can wrap your head around rather than unrealistic goals that produce stress, worry, and fear throughout the journey because you have no idea how you're going to achieve them. Goal-setting should be an exciting process, not a burden. When setting unrealistic goals, all that usually brings are negative emotions, which then transmute into physical symptoms—worry because you're not sure how you're going to do it; therefore, you experience headaches; stress because every day that passes, your deadline is closer and you're not even close to achieving it; and anxiety because you have no idea what the next steps are, and you fear feeling like a failure if you don't accomplish them. It is important to relax and breathe throughout the process. Set goals that feel achievable but are still a challenge. Refrain from setting goals that are challenging but produce negative BS every time you think about them.

The Pros

- **Your goals are clear and concise.** As your goals are specific, you know exactly where you want to go without having to question it or overthink. When we have clear and specific goals, it feels easier to accomplish. We're not questioning the validity of our goals, nor are we questioning what the next steps are. We know what to do, when to do it, and how to do it.

- **Visualizing feels easy.** When you create SMART goals, you are able to clearly visualize what your unique success looks like. Because your visualization is strong, you're able to manifest your dreams quicker than having to overthink and second guess everything. Visualization is an important key to goal-setting effectiveness.

- **Large goals can be broken down.** When goal-setting, you can reverse engineer the process. You have an opportunity to take large goals and break them down into bite-sized pieces that are easier to swallow. By doing this, your goals feel realistic to achieve and you learn to enjoy the process. You feel peace and joy and you simply live in the moment.

- **You can take your time.** Creating SMART goals is an individual journey. You don't need to rush; you can take as much time as you need to accomplish your goals. If it helps, you can also complete one goal at a time, so you don't feel overwhelmed and burned out. Goal-setting can fit into your lifestyle as much as you'd like to, which makes the process even more enjoyable.

- **Life lessons can be learned daily.** One of the most powerful things about setting SMART goals is that there are always lessons you can learn. You become mindful of mistakes you make and aware of how to rectify them immediately. You learn about yourself and your inner power as you understand what challenges you, excites you, and makes you feel overwhelmed. You also learn about your own boundaries and the importance of holding yourself accountable in accomplishing your goals. If you don't achieve them by the deadline, you can dive deeper into understanding why, so you can rectify it for your next goal.

Asking For Support

When creating SMART goals, it may not feel easy to accomplish on your own. Distractions can get in the way, excuses may show up, and negative BS may try to control your mind. It is important to ask for help and support when this happens, otherwise you may feel the best thing to do is quit, and everything you've accomplished thus far goes down the drain.

There are many people you can ask for support from:

- **Partners.** Your spouse can be a great support for you during goal-setting. They can help hold you accountable (similar to a spotter at the gym), prepare meals or help clean the house when you're on the verge of hitting a milestone, take care of the kids when you're in the middle of a task, or listen to you vent about your challenges and offer advice when needed. There are many ways your partner can show their support; it's a matter of asking them for help when you need it.

- **Coaches and mentors.** These are great individuals to ask for support from. They can offer an unbiased opinion of your challenges and help you navigate the process as you dismantle the struggles you're facing. As they are part of your external support team, they will tell you things that you need to hear, rather than spare your feelings. This will help you with your personal and professional growth.

- **Friends or co-workers.** As you have a strong relationship with many of your friends and colleagues, they can certainly feel like your guide when you are losing hope. Most of your friends will offer you an unbiased opinion when you need assistance, as they will offer an open thought that someone close to you, such as your partner, may not be able to offer you. A lot of the time, they'll usually tell you exactly how it is in a way that may kick you in the butt, but it's all in the name of love and unconditional support.

- **Yourself.** This may sound funny but writing in your journal can offer amazing support as you navigate your growth. Your inner self goes through the process with you; therefore, it is important that you speak to them daily. They know you and your goals better than anyone else. By journaling, you can discover a whole new side of you that's been hidden due to fear, worry, or anxiety.

- **Your spiritual team.** As the universe partners with you to make your goals happen, it is important you reach out by faith and ask for their help every day. Express gratitude for accomplishing your goals, even before they happen, and ask for guidance as you learn to navigate difficult challenges.

- **Guidance counselor or therapist.** When you have trouble navigating challenges on your own and you don't feel any support from friends or family, these are great people to connect with. Their knowledge and expertise can help you through the process, as you learn to understand where triggers are coming from and how to let them go gracefully so you can move forward with peace, joy, and happiness.

- **Accountability partners.** They can be your best friend, spouse, parent, co-worker, sibling, or business associate. Having an accountability partner during goal-setting can be quite effective, as they are meant to hold you accountable when you lack motivation. They support you by ensuring your tasks are completed, and they may even give you a little pep talk when you feel like procrastinating or feel uninspired.

Taking Inspired Action

When wanting to set goals and achieve them, taking action cannot be taken lightly. Many of us desire to accomplish our goals, but if we don't take actionable steps to get there, they'll never come into fruition, or the process will take longer than expected. We'll scratch our head wondering why things aren't working. This is when we need to hold ourselves accountable and honor what we said we are going to do in the time we said we're going to do it.

I like to think of this step as taking *inspired* action, rather than only taking action. By taking action, you're only doing. The steps don't excite you, and you do them because you have to, not because there is a greater purpose involved. By taking *inspired* action, motivation is at the forefront of your goals. You take the steps you need to take, but you complete them with passion, excitement, and alignment. You take the step because it feels like it's the right step to take. You listen and trust your intuition, and you feel peace with each action you take.

In order to take inspired action, you can follow these steps:

Journal About Your Goals

Writing them down not only helps solidify them and holds you accountable but allows you to be crystal clear with which goals you want to achieve. When they're not written down, they stay stuck in our mind, and by human nature, we forget about accomplishing them. Recall the saying 'Out of sight, out of mind?' (Heywood, 1546).

When you write them down, you accomplish a few things:

- **A commitment to yourself.** Writing them down is like a written contract that you set with yourself. By reading your goals to yourself, you keep yourself accountable and honor the commitment in accomplishing them.

- **Subconscious re-wiring.** Writing your goals down can help instill the commitment in your subconscious mind. It will help release any negative BS your subconscious mind is holding onto and help reframe any beliefs that may keep you stuck during the process.

- **Focus.** It is important to write and read your goals every day, even multiple times throughout the day, as doing this will help keep your focus and dedication intact. This is very effective, especially if you attach your reasons to your goals. You remind yourself of why you're setting the goals in the first place, which keeps you motivated and inspired.

Set Your Deadline

Creating a timeline for your goals is crucial for effective goal-setting. By creating deadlines for when you want to achieve your goals, you remain focused and don't allow anything (or anyone) to distract you during the process. It's as if you're preparing a project for school. You're the teacher and the student at the same time. As the teacher, you offer a deadline for when the project needs to be completed, and as the student, you do everything in your power to meet that deadline.

If you don't set a deadline for yourself, your commitment and honor to your goals become wasted. Without a deadline, you stay in your comfort zone, relaxing and barely taking action. There is no sense of urgency; in your mind, you can accomplish it whenever you feel like it. With a deadline, you feel a sense of urgency, as every day, the date gets closer; therefore, you learn to take daily inspired action, rather than let the day go by.

Reframe Your Mindset

Mindset work is one of the most, if not the most, powerful piece for your success. If you don't work on your mindset consistently, it will be a lonely and self-sabotaging process. You procrastinate all the time, negative BS controls your life, self-trust and commitment is lost, and motivation is lacking. By working on your mindset every day, you can reframe it for positivity that inspires and lights you up, rather than constantly makes you feel like a failure or an imposter as you attempt to accomplish a task

The First Step Matters

This may sound a bit cliché, but the first step is the one that matters the most. It is also the hardest step to take. For example, if one of your goals is to skydive, and you're in the plane ready to jump, the instructor usually says this: "The hardest part is letting go." This is the same with goal-setting. The hardest part is always taking the first step. At times, we may not have the courage to begin taking action because we fear we're not good enough, or we may feel like people will judge us;

therefore, subconsciously, we prefer to hide and stay small.

By pushing away your fear and mustering up the courage to take the first step toward your goals, you're already successful. You've already pushed past the hardest threshold. Once you let go of the airplane, it'll feel like smooth sailing from there.

Keep Going

Just because you take the first step, doesn't mean you can sit back and relax. Keep taking inspired action until you reach your goals. Even then, I encourage you to keep going. Find ways to innovate so you keep strengthening your mindset after each goal, so you don't stay stagnant and comfortable. If you choose to sit back and relax after every step you take, the journey will feel longer to complete. Motivate yourself to keep taking action, no matter how it may feel.

Celebrate Your Accomplishments

You've done it. You've accomplished your goals. Congratulations! It is important that you celebrate, no matter how big or small your goals are. When you continually celebrate, more accomplishments come your way. Celebration is a part of abundant energy; the energy you need to be in to receive more things to celebrate and express gratitude for. Full disclaimer: Your reward doesn't have to be fancy. It can be something as simple as taking a bubble bath and relaxing or making your family a delicious dinner. The way you choose to reward yourself and celebrate is perfect.

Chapter Eight Soulwork

As we've spoken all throughout this chapter, our goals will only feel effective when we take inspired action every day. Not weekly; every day. The more we take action, the quicker it'll be for our goals to come into fruition, and we can celebrate.

That being said, it's time to take some inspired action.

In your journal, set a goal for yourself. It can be anything–relationships, financial, career, personal–but remember to make it achievable, realistic, and specific. Once you have a goal in mind, use the SMART method and write down your goals. Break them down into bite-sized pieces so they feel more achievable to accomplish.

Once you've made your goal a SMART one, note any negative BS that may come up when thinking about your goal:

I'm too old

I'm not enough

I'm not worthy

I don't have the skills or knowledge

I have no time

Who am I to think it can happen?

Once you're mindful of these limiting beliefs, you can counteract them with a positive BS that will help you move forward.

The last step of this soulwork is to decide what you determine as success. In your journal, ask yourself these questions:

- When I achieve my goal, how will I feel?

- What part of my goal will already make me feel successful before I even achieve it?

- What will motivate me to work on my goal until I achieve it? Conclusion: Your Accountability Contract

Accountability is the glue that ties commitment to the result. –
Bob Proctor

Living life with integrity is not always easy, especially in times of overwhelm.

You can do all the things and say all the things that make you feel better but feeling like an imposter just doesn't seem to quit. All of the negative emotions surface again and again, and it always feels like a never-ending cycle, throwing you around like a washing machine that never turns off.

You've just completed this book. Now it's up to you. Are you ready to hold yourself accountable, or do you prefer to stay in your little turtle shell and only come out when it's safe to do so?

You don't have to be stuck in that shell forever. You can come out, play, and make mistakes like the rest of us and still come out positively on the other side. Life doesn't always have to be about feeling like an imposter. You can feel like a winner at any moment.

We've spoken about so many things in this book. Feel free to read it again and again. If you desire clarity in a specific section, jump to that section, read it again, and dive deeper into the soulwork at the end.

As a brief overview, here are some highlights you can take with you as you go through your journey:

- The first step is always the hardest one to take, but it is the one that matters most. Don't be scared to jump off the airplane. Learn to let go so you can move forward.

- Keep pushing forward, no matter what. There may be times when imposter syndrome shows its ugly face; don't give it the glory. Move forward taking uncomfortable, imperfect actions every day. It gets easier over time.

- Celebrate even if your dreams are small. Rewarding yourself after every accomplishment will keep you motivated, regardless of how big or small the goal is. By praising yourself, you will step forward into the next goal with encouragement and dedication.

- Do your mindset work every day. As we've spoken, reframing your mindset is important for your success.

- Define your success in a way that feels right to you. Success is an inside game. It's not a competition toward the finish line.

- Use tools such as the Emotion Wheel to help you surpass any challenges. They are there to aid you in creating a deeper relationship with yourself, where you can experience constant growth and learn from your mistakes.

- Keep evolving and innovating. There is never any growth in staying in your comfort zone and staying in a fixed, stagnant mindset. Trust the process and keep growing every day.

- You are the CEO of your own success. You have the power to make things happen at the time you choose to.

- Imposter syndrome doesn't need to stay in your life forever. You can take back control of your own life by simply focusing on what matters.

- Break your glass ceiling again and again. Every level of growth requires a harder ceiling to break. Trust yourself and honor your commitment to breaking them down. You can do this!

Growing up, my mom used to say, "You're only as good as your word." I understand that I am making a pretty big assumption when I say this, but most of us do whatever we can to try and keep our promises to others. We go about our day, saying yes and making promises to our partner, children, coworkers, and friends:

Don't forget to pick up the drycleaning.

Can you pick up some milk on the way home?

Can you help me with my homework?

I have a big project that is due. Can I run it by you to see what you think?

We're all going out for our friend's birthday on Saturday. Are you coming? We'd love to see you!

We make so many promises and commit to others as much as we can, but yet, we still feel like imposters and overthink about whether we are enough.

As you think about this, I want to ask you something:

If we do everything in our power to keep our word to others, why don't we do it for ourselves? We hold ourselves accountable in honoring our word when it comes to helping others, but how come we don't do the same for our own goals?

So often, it feels so easy to start a project and never complete it or cancel our self-care plans so we can cover someone else at work. To be fair, when it comes down to it, it feels easier to disappoint ourselves rather than disappoint others.

That being said, it's important to keep in integrity with ourselves throughout this process. So, how can we do this? By setting ourselves up with a strong accountability system. This system will aid in not only holding yourself accountable, but it will help you to successfully accomplish your goals.

There are many tools and resources that you can implement. We spoke about a few throughout the book:

- block out time on your calendar and no matter what, DO NOT MOVE IT
- set reminders on your phone
- find a coach to check in with
- find a support group
- create your own support group with a book club
- talk to a partner or friend that you trust

As you move forward with overcoming your worst enemy, I encourage you to find an accountability tool that resonates with you and challenges you at the same time. Please remember that you do not have to stay stuck in imposter syndrome. You always have the choice to get yourself out of it at any time you wish.

If you know of anyone who can benefit from reading this book–maybe your partner, friend, colleague, or client–please give them this book as a token of appreciation to show them that you care about their well-being and their success. They will appreciate it more than you know.

Thanks for reading.

Passion Over Perfection,

Sydney Jackson-Clockston

Share This Book With Others

Your book was awesome! This book is about imposter syndrome, how one is affected when experiencing it, ways to navigate it, and how to build a sustainable plan of action when it comes up. The book is straightforward, has excellent journal questions to work with, and is easy to understand and put into practice.

I enjoyed reading and wanted more, but also super happy at the quick read. I 100% want to use it for supervision with my staff and coworkers as well as my mentees.

Mayra Aviña, MSW
Senior Manager in Family Support Services
And Owner of Cempaxochilt Arts

If you're looking for a book to push you forward in growth to achieve what you feel is unachievable, this is the one. In My Own Worst Enemy: Understanding and Overcoming Imposter Syndrome, Jackson-Clockston shares her experiences alongside inspiration and action steps for how to heal from imposter syndrome and reclaim your ability to be unstoppable. Through her writing, Jackson-Clockston gives you permission to step into your own greatness by discovering what makes you unique and trusting yourself and your dreams. Her clear breakdown of what she's learned on her own journey sets a framework for the soulwork and journal prompts for going "all in" on your own self-exploration. If you're ready to get uncomfortable, the interactive portions of the book allow you to recognize and understand your own limiting belief systems, where you're holding yourself back, and how to take steps to change your mindset. Aptly describing this book as a "success toolkit," Jackson-Clockston's thought-provoking questions allow you to dive deep into the systems and structures currently framing your life while providing immediately applicable guidance for working through your own imposter syndrome and insecurities. Make sure you have a journal and pen at the ready because this book is going to make you THINK!

There is so much power emanating from Jackson-Clockston's words! I didn't know how much I needed to read this book until I got into its pages. It was the "get back on track" push I was looking for to move forward with some of my own entrepreneurial goals. Whether in reading this book, actively doing the soulwork, or passively going about my day, I found myself recognizing when I needed to step back and pause, BREATHE, and think about what Jackson-Clockston had written. What was I feeling? How could I sit in a moment with myself, give myself grace for those feelings, and then move on to find my direction again? The immediate applicability of Jackson-Clockston's writing is Empowering.

I cannot wait to buy this book for my own accountability partners so we can work on building our individual strengths, getting over imposter syndrome, and encouraging each other toward our goals.

Alissa M. Trumbull

I just finished reading your book. There are many things I like about the book- I love the conversational style. It made me feel comfortable immediately. I like the format of an exercise at the end of each chapter. It pushes the reader to do something with what they have just read.

The book, to me, presents as mostly about awareness, with some tools to help the reader find ways to overcome imposter syndrome. I envision it being a go-to short read for anyone who thinks they are an imposter. It could be a handy reference.

With love,
Jeanne

This book is unique because it not only breaks down different definitions of imposter syndrome but also gives examples to help overcome the negative thoughts we all sometimes have. I liked how the book gives different ways to help you find support and accountability for yourself to be as successful as you can be

This book is for readers looking for self-motivation, self-love, and who want to learn how to take accountability for lack of confidence in themselves

Kathern Johnson Owner of
Black Vision Vill

Sydney Jackson- Clockston's book is easy to read, even for beginners, but profound enough to help even an accomplished academic, like myself, understand the subtle ways that Imposter Syndrome may be intruding upon one's life and thoughts. Sydney is able to teach us how to use journaling as a simple yet effective tool in our self-care toolbox, including how to use journaling to become more self-aware and to use our own self-awareness to overcome the self-sabotage that Imposter Syndrome wreaks upon our lives. You may be surprised to find the ways this relates to you, even if you thought this could not possibly be affecting you. As you go through her book, she offers many examples of questions you might ask yourself to get you thinking in a new way about your life, your thoughts, and the stories you have been telling yourself. Her book is a must read for anyone who is curious about Imposter Syndrome or is unsure whether they may or may not be affected by it. I suggest taking your time with this book. It is meant to be reflective, and to lead you to your own inner truth. Sydney is naturally gifted at encouraging and empowering you to take an honest look at what is really there in your heart and mind and to breathe life into yourself again through authentic recognition of your feelings, acceptance of yourself as you are, and intentionally shifting your thoughts and stories to reflect the person you are becoming. It is a must-read for anyone who has that niggling inner voice of self-doubt or anyone looking for tools to let go and step into the fullness of who you really are. Highly recommended!

Tamara Love
Owner of Prayer Craft

Glossary

- **Accountability:** The process where you learn to take responsibility for your own actions.

- **Affirmations:** A cluster of positive, uplifting statements that help increase your confidence and self-love.

- **Belief System (BS):** A set of beliefs, either positive or negative, that influence the way people make decisions. These beliefs form during childhood and tend to influence a person's character, actions, and behaviors.

- **External Validation:** Desiring people's love, support, and affection and longing for them to tell you how worthy you are. These people are the ones who delegate your decisions, as you are not comfortable making them yourself.

- **Fear of Failure:** A sense of worry that, when you finally achieve success, it will be stripped away from you, and you'll feel like a failure.

- **Fear of Success:** A sense of worry that, when you achieve your own version of success, you will be taken advantage of or treated differently by friends or loved ones.

- **Fixed Mindset:** When your mind feels stagnant and comfortable. It continues with the same behaviors and actions, intending to never move forward.

- **Goal-Setting:** Creating an achievable and realistic outcome that helps you move forward, while striving for a better life.

- **Goals:** Realistic and achievable expectations that, when you accomplish them, feel like success.

- **Growth Mindset:** When the mind has an opportunity to transform and renew itself. The mind seeks new opportunities in order to sprout a new way of living.

- **Imposter Syndrome:** An emotional rollercoaster of negative feelings and thoughts that continually tell you that you are not enough as you are. Constant doubt and lack of confidence is imminent; feeling like a failure is the norm, despite the credentials and accomplishments you've already obtained.

- **Integrity:** The quality of being honest and having strong moral principles; moral uprightness. The state of being whole and undivided.

- **Mindfulness:** An opportunity for personal growth, where you are simply focusing on being aware of the present moment in your life and enjoying what it has to offer you.

- **People-Pleaser:** The YES person. The one that does everything for everybody and neglects themselves. The one that can feel burned out at times, but still makes promises to others and keeps them. A people-pleaser usually does things for everyone in order to be liked, as they dislike feeling unloved.

- **Perfectionism:** Wanting everything in your life to feel perfect without any flaws or imperfections. Striving for a life that doesn't exist.

- **Self-Accountability:** Holding yourself in integrity to do the things you say you are going to do. Honoring your word, no matter what. Your word is law.

- **Self-Trust:** Being able to be confident in your own abilities so you can achieve the success you're longing for, despite any challenges and obstacles that may arise.

- **Soulwork:** Another name for homework but completed with purpose and intention. Helping you find a way to BE, rather than simply DO.

- **Subconscious Mind:** The part of your mind that controls about 95% of your decision-making. The part that is not visible to the naked eye, but it is the most powerful to your personal growth.

- **Uniqueness:** A sense of inner belonging that your higher self knows as your truth. You are free to be you every single day.

References

BetterHelp Editorial Team. (2022, October 6). *What Is Imposter Syndrome and How to Overcome It.* betterhelp.com. https://www.betterhelp.com/advice/careers/what-is-imposter-syndrome-and-how-to-overcome-it/?utm_source=AdWords&utm_medium=Search_PPC_c&utm_term=PerformanceMax&utm_content=&network=x&placement=&target=&matchtype=&utm_campaign=17990185911&ad_type=responsive_pmax&adposition=&gclid=Cj0KCQiAmaibBhCAARIsAKUlaKT-jqFaep54Li8jFvTB_uwFY8RFxPwaEusHPJBeKIVlb7z2QLGhFUcaAslpEALw_wcB

Bothello, J. (2022, January 26). *Who Is Most Susceptible to Imposter Syndrome? | The Walrus.* Thewalrus.ca. https://thewalrus.ca/s3e15-joel-bothello-the-conversation-piece/?gclid=Cj0KCQiAmaibBhCAARIsAKUlaKR2bxa3MpOhAncrBFheJ0c4J89p_q6icFOd5n2HNgKrPYQHuICuEjkaAtMIEALw_wcB

Butterfly Life Cycle. (n.d.). Ansp.org. https://ansp.org/exhibits/online-exhibits/butterflies/lifecycle/#:~:text=Butterflies%2C%20moths%2C%20beetles%2C%20flies

Cooper, B. (2017, August 31). *Imposter Syndrome: Why You Have It and What You Can Do About It.* Zapier.com. https://zapier.com/blog/what-is-imposter-syndrome/

Cote, C. (2022, March 10). *Growth Mindset vs. Fixed Mindset: What's the Difference?.* Business Insights Blog. https://online.hbs.edu/blog/post/growth-mindset-vs-fixed-mindset#:~:text=Someone%20with%20a%20growth%20mindset

Cuncic, A. (2022, November 7). *What Is Imposter Syndrome?.* Verywellmind.com. https://www.verywellmind.com/imposter-syndrome-and-social-anxiety-disorder-4156469

Davis, T. (n.d.). *Emotion: Definition, Theories, and List of Emotions.* The Berkeley Well-Being Institute. https://www.berkeleywellbeing.com/emotion.html

Definition of Control. (2019). Merriam-Webster.com. https://www.merriam-webster.com/dictionary/control

Germino, D. (2020, July 23). *How to Crush Your Limiting Beliefs and Reach Your True Potential.* Happiness in

Training. https://medium.com/happiness-in-training/how-to-crush-your-limiting-beliefs-and-reach-your-true-potential-3d0fae352abb

Gurteen, D. (2022, April 1). *Belief systems*. Conversational Leadership. https://conversational-leadership.net/belief-systems/#:~:text=A%20belief%20system%20is%20a

Indeed Editorial Team. (2021, January 5). *15 Ways To Define Personal Success*. Indeed Career Guide. https://www.indeed.com/career-advice/interviewing/define-success

Klynn, B. (2021, June 22). *Emotional regulation: Skills, exercises, and strategies*. Betterup.com. https://www.betterup.com/blog/emotional-regulation-skills

Leonard, J. (2020, September 17). *Impostor syndrome: Symptoms, types, and how to deal with it*. medicalnewstoday.com.https://www.medicalnewstoday.com/articles/321730#:~:text=Impostor%20syndrome%20can%20affect%20anyone

Mind Tools Content Team. (n.d.). *Locus of Control*. Mindtools.com. https://www.mindtools.com/am8v6ux/locus-of-control

Mind Tools Content Team. (n.d.). *SMART Goals*. Mindtools.com. https://www.mindtools.com/a4wo118/smart-goals

Nance-Nash, S. (2020, July 28). *Why imposter syndrome hits women and women of colour harder*. Bbc.com, https://www.bbc.com/worklife/article/20200724-why-imposter-syndrome-hits-women-and-women-of-colour-harder

Nguyen, J. (2021, May 23). *This Therapist-Approved Tool Is So Useful For Understanding Your Emotions*. Mindbodygreen. https://www.mindbodygreen.com/articles/emotion-wheel

9 interesting facts about your subconscious mind - Gail Marra Hypnotherapy. (2021, November 11). https://www.gailmarrahypnotherapy.com/9-interesting-facts-about-your-subconscious-mind/#:~:text=The%20Subconscious%20Mind%20controls%2095%20percent%20of%20your%20life&text=Todays%20science%20estimates%20that%2095

Ralph, L. (2018, October 7). *What Actually Is a Belief? and Why Is It so Hard to Change?*. Psychology Today. https://www.psychologytoday.com/us/blog/finding-purpose/201810/what-actually-is-belief-and-why-is-it-so-hard-change

Reddy, K. (2016, June 29). *S.M.A.R.T Goals: Definition, Importance, Advantages & Disadvantages.* WiseStep. https://content.wisestep.com/smart-goals-definition-importance-advantages-disadvantages/

Usher, I. (2014, August 13). *Seven simple steps to achieving all of your goals.* Virgin.com. https://www.virgin.com/about-virgin/latest/seven-simple-steps-to-achieving-all-of-your-goals

Weir, K. (2013). *Feel like a fraud?.* Apa.org. https://www.apa.org/gradpsych/2013/11/fraud

Wilding, Melody. (2017, May 10). *5 Different Types of Imposter Syndrome (and 5 Ways to Battle Each One).* The Muse. https://www.themuse.com/advice/5-different-types-of-imposter-syndrome-and-5-ways-to-battle-each-one

www.ingramcontent.com/pod-product-compliance
Lightning Source LLC
Chambersburg PA
CBHW031632160426
43196CB00006B/378